VB.NET AND SQL CLIENT

Working with the Dataview

Richard Thomas Edwards

CONTENTS

Welcome To SQLCLIENT
What is SQLCLIENT

THE FIRST THING THAT SHOULD POP OUT AT YOU IS THE FACT THAT THIS ENTIRE BOOK IS DEDICATED TO THE USE OF THE DATAVIEW. The others will be covered in separate books. So, what is SQL Client?

SQL Client is a dedicated suite of objects designed specifically for SQL Server. Unlike OLEDB where providers including the existing SQL Server Provider – SQLOLEDB – works with OLEDB. The reverse is not true. Same thing goes for ODBC. While there is a driver for SQL Server, that is only one of many ODBC drivers that can be used with ODBC.

The SQLCLIENT Objects
Connection, Command DataReader and
DataAdapter

F YOU HAVE BEEN WORKING WITH .NET FOR SOME TIME AND HAVE BEEN WORKING WITH SQLCLIENT, ODBC, OR SQL CLIENT, YOU KNOW THEY ALL LOOK PRETTY MUCH THE SAME. You have the connection; the command; and you populate the information using a DataReader or A DataAdapter. Below, is pretty much how all of it works together:

```
Dim cnstr As String = ""
Dim strQuery As String = ""
```

Connection, Command and DataAdapter

```
Dim cn as new System.Data.SQLClient.SQLClientConnection()
Cn.ConnectionString = cnstr
Cn.Open()

Dim cmd as new System.Data.SQLClient.SQLClientCommand()
Cmd.Connection = cn
Cmd.CommandType = CommandTypeText
```

```
Cmd.ExecuteNonQuery()

Dim DA as System.Data.SQLClient.SQLClientDataAdatper(cmd)
```

Connection and DataAdapter

```
Dim cn as new System.Data.SQLClient.SQLClientConnection()
Cn.ConnectionString = cnstr
Cn.Open()

Dim DA as System.Data.SQLClient.SQLClientDataAdatper(strQuery, cn)
```

Command and DataAdapter

```
Dim cmd as new System.Data.SQLClient.SQLClientCommand()
Cmd.Connection =  new System.Data.SQLClient.SQLClientConnection
Cmd.Connection.ConnectionString = cnstr
Cmd.Connection.Open()
Cmd.CommandType = CommandTypeText
Cmd.ExecuteNonQuery()

Dim DA as System.Data.SQLClient.SQLClientDataAdatper(cmd)
```

DataAdapter

```
Dim DA as System.Data.SQLClient.SQLClientDataAdatper(strQuery, cnstr)
```

Connection, Command and DataReader

```
Dim cn as new System.Data.SQLClient.SQLClientConnection()
Cn.ConnectionString = cnstr
```

Cn.Open()

Dim cmd as new System.Data.SQLClient.SQLClientCommand()
Cmd.Connection = cn
Cmd.CommandType = CommandTypeText
Dim dr As System.Data.SQLClient.SQLClientDataReader = cmd.ExecuteReader()

Command and Reader

Dim cmd as new System.Data.SQLClient.SQLClientCommand()
Cmd.Connection = new System.Data.SQLClient.SQLClientConnection
Cmd.Connection.ConnectionString = cnstr
Cmd.Connection.Open()
Cmd.CommandType = CommandTypeText
Dim dr As System.Data.SQLClient.SQLClientDataReader = cmd.ExecuteReader()

Working with the DataTable
Bound or unbound

THIS MAY COME A SURPRISE TO YOU BUT THE DATATABLE CAN BE POPULATED AS A BOUND OBJECT OR AN UNBOUND OBJECT. Let's start with the normal way first and then I'll show you how it can be used in the unbound mode.

Okay, so you have an SQLDataAdapter filled with the information you want to bind to the System.Data.DataTable.

Dim dt as new System.Data.DataTable
DA.Fill(dt)
You can also specify the tablename here, too.
DA.Fill(dt)
Dt.Tablename = ""

Now, you have a DataTable simply do the following:

DataGridView1.DataSource = dt.DefaultView

That will populate the DataGridView.

Doing it Manually

```vbnet
Dim dt As New System.Data.DataTable()
Dim dv As System.Data.DataView = dt.DefaultView
Dim svc As Object = GetObject("winmgmts:\\.\Root\CIMV2")
Dim objs = svc.InstancesOf("Win32_Process")
For Each obj In objs
    For Each prop As Object In obj.Properties_
        dv.Table.Columns.Add(prop.Name,
GetType(System.String))
    Next
    Exit For
Next

Dim x As Integer = 0
Dim y As Integer = 0

For Each obj In objs
    dv.Table.Rows.Add()
    For Each prop As Object In obj.Properties_
        dv.Table.Rows(y).Item(prop.Name) =
GetValue(prop.Name, obj)
    Next
    y = y + 1
Next

DataGridView1.DataSource = dt.DefaultView


Public Function GetValue(ByVal name As String, ByVal obj As
Object) As String

    Dim pos As Integer = InStr(obj.GetObjectText_, vbTab &
name & " = ")

    If pos Then

        Dim tempstr As String = Mid(obj.GetObjectText_, pos +
Len(name & " = "), Len(obj.GetObjectText_))
        pos = InStr(tempstr, ";")
```

```
            tempstr = Mid$(tempstr, 1, pos - 1)
            tempstr = Replace(tempstr, Chr(34), "")
            tempstr = Replace(tempstr, "{", "")
            tempstr = Replace(tempstr, "}", "")
            If tempstr.Length > 14 Then
                If obj.Properties_.Item(name).CIMType = 101 Then
                    tempstr = Mid(tempstr, 5, 2) & "/" & _
                              Mid(tempstr, 7, 2) & "/" & _
                              Mid(tempstr, 1, 4) & " " & _
                              Mid(tempstr, 9, 2) & ":" & _
                              Mid(tempstr, 11, 2) & ":" & _
                              Mid(tempstr, 13, 2)
                End If
            End If
            GetValue = tempstr
        Else
            GetValue = ""
        End If

End Function
```

ASP Examples

BELOW ARE EXAMPLES OF SQLCLIENT USING A DATATABLE.

Reports

Horizontal

```
Dim cnstr as String = ""
Dim strQuery as String = ""

Dim cn As System.Data.SQLClient.SQLClientConnection  = new
System.Data.SQLClient.SQLClientConnection(cnstr)
cn.Open()

Dim cmd As System.Data.SQLClient.SQLClientCommand  = new
System.Data.SQLClient.SQLClientCommand()
cmd.Connection = cn
cmd.CommandType = 1
cmd.CommandText = strQuery
cmd.ExecuteNonquery()

Dim da As System.Data.SQLClient.SQLClientDataAdapter  = new
System.Data.SQLClient.SQLClientDataAdapter(cmd)
```

```
Dim dt as new System.Data.DataTable
da.Fill(dt)

Dim dv as System.Data.DataView = dt.DefaultView

Dim ws As Object  = CreateObject("WScript.Shell")
Dim fso As Object  = CreateObject("Scripting.FileSystemObject")
Dim txtstream as Object  = fso.OpenTextFile(ws.CurrentDirectory +
"\Products.asp", 2, true, -2)
txtstream.WriteLine("<hmtl>")
txtstream.WriteLine("<head>")
txtstream.WriteLine("<title>Products</title>")
txtstream.WriteLine("<style type='text/css'>")
txtstream.WriteLine("th")
txtstream.WriteLine("{")
txtstream.WriteLine("    COLOR: darkred;")
txtstream.WriteLine("    BACKGROUND-COLOR: #eeeeee;")
txtstream.WriteLine("    FONT-FAMILY: Cambria, serif;")
txtstream.WriteLine("    FONT-SIZE: 12px;")
txtstream.WriteLine("    text-align: left;")
txtstream.WriteLine("    white-Space: nowrap='nowrap';")
txtstream.WriteLine("}")
txtstream.WriteLine("td")
txtstream.WriteLine("{")
txtstream.WriteLine("    COLOR: navy;")
txtstream.WriteLine("    BACKGROUND-COLOR: #eeeeee;")
txtstream.WriteLine("    FONT-FAMILY: Cambria, serif;")
txtstream.WriteLine("    FONT-SIZE: 12px;")
txtstream.WriteLine("    text-align: left;")
txtstream.WriteLine("    white-Space: nowrap='nowrap';")
txtstream.WriteLine("}")
txtstream.WriteLine("</style>")

txtstream.WriteLine("</head>")
txtstream.WriteLine("<body>")
txtstream.WriteLine("<center>")
txtstream.WriteLine("</br>")
```

```
txtstream.WriteLine("<table border=0 cellspacing=3 cellpadding=3>")
txtstream.WriteLine("<%")
txtstream.WriteLine("Response.Write(""<tr>"" & vbcrlf)")
For Each col as System.Data.DataColumn in dv.Table.Columns
txtstream.WriteLine("Response.Write(""<th align='left'
nowrap='nowrap'>" & col.Caption & "</th>"" & vbcrlf)")
Next
txtstream.WriteLine("Response.Write(""</tr>"" & vbcrlf)")

for each row as System.Data.DataRow in dv.Table.Rows
txtstream.WriteLine("Response.Write(""<tr>"" & vbcrlf)")
For Each col as System.Data.DataColumn in dv.Table.Columns
txtstream.WriteLine("Response.Write(""<td  align='left'
nowrap='nowrap'>" & row.Item(col.Caption) & "</td>"" & vbcrlf)")
Next

txtstream.WriteLine("Response.Write(""</tr>"" & vbcrlf)")

Next
txtstream.WriteLine("%>")
txtstream.WriteLine("</table>")
txtstream.WriteLine("</body>")
txtstream.WriteLine("</html>")
txtstream.Close()




        Vertical


Dim cnstr as String = ""
Dim strQuery as String = ""

Dim cn As System.Data.SQLClient.SQLClientConnection  = new
System.Data.SQLClient.SQLClientConnection(cnstr)
cn.Open()
```

```
Dim cmd As System.Data.SQLClient.SQLClientCommand  = new
System.Data.SQLClient.SQLClientCommand()
cmd.Connection = cn
cmd.CommandType = 1
cmd.CommandText = strQuery
cmd.ExecuteNonquery()

Dim da As System.Data.SQLClient.SQLClientDataAdapter  = new
System.Data.SQLClient.SQLClientDataAdapter(cmd)

Dim dt as new System.Data.DataTable
da.Fill(dt)

Dim dv as System.Data.DataView = dt.DefaultView

Dim ws As Object  = CreateObject("WScript.Shell")
Dim fso As Object  = CreateObject("Scripting.FileSystemObject")
Dim txtstream as Object  = fso.OpenTextFile(ws.CurrentDirectory +
"\Products.asp", 2, true, -2)
txtstream.WriteLine("<hmtl>")
txtstream.WriteLine("<head>")
txtstream.WriteLine("<title>Products</title>")
txtstream.WriteLine("<style type='text/css'>")
txtstream.WriteLine("th")
txtstream.WriteLine(" {")
txtstream.WriteLine("    COLOR: darkred;")
txtstream.WriteLine("    BACKGROUND-COLOR: #eeeeee;")
txtstream.WriteLine("    FONT-FAMILY: Cambria, serif;")
txtstream.WriteLine("    FONT-SIZE: 12px;")
txtstream.WriteLine("    text-align: left;")
txtstream.WriteLine("    white-Space: nowrap='nowrap';")
txtstream.WriteLine("}")
txtstream.WriteLine("td")
txtstream.WriteLine(" {")
txtstream.WriteLine("    COLOR: navy;")
txtstream.WriteLine("    BACKGROUND-COLOR: #eeeeee;")
txtstream.WriteLine("    FONT-FAMILY: Cambria, serif;")
```

```
txtstream.WriteLine("    FONT-SIZE: 12px;")
txtstream.WriteLine("    text-align: left;")
txtstream.WriteLine("    white-Space: nowrap='nowrap';")
txtstream.WriteLine("}")
txtstream.WriteLine("</style>")

txtstream.WriteLine("</head>")
txtstream.WriteLine("<body>")
txtstream.WriteLine("<center>")
txtstream.WriteLine("</br>")
txtstream.WriteLine("<table border=0 cellspacing=3 cellpadding=3>")
txtstream.WriteLine("<%")
For Each col as System.Data.DataColumn in dv.Table.Columns
txtstream.WriteLine("Response.Write(""<tr><th align='left'
nowrap='nowrap'>" & col.Caption & "</th>"" & vbcrlf)")
for each row as System.Data.DataRow in dv.Table.Rows
txtstream.WriteLine("Response.Write(""<td  align='left'
nowrap='true'><input type=text value=""" & row.Item(col.Caption) &
"""></input></td>"" & vbcrlf)")

Next
txtstream.WriteLine("Response.Write(""</tr>"" & vbcrlf)")
Next
txtstream.WriteLine("%>")
txtstream.WriteLine("</table>")
txtstream.WriteLine("</body>")
txtstream.WriteLine("</html>")
txtstream.Close()
```

Tables

Horizontal

```
Dim cnstr as String = ""
Dim strQuery as String = ""

Dim cn As System.Data.SQLClient.SQLClientConnection  = new
System.Data.SQLClient.SQLClientConnection(cnstr)
cn.Open()

Dim cmd As System.Data.SQLClient.SQLClientCommand  = new
System.Data.SQLClient.SQLClientCommand()
cmd.Connection = cn
cmd.CommandType = 1
cmd.CommandText = strQuery
cmd.ExecuteNonquery()

Dim da As System.Data.SQLClient.SQLClientDataAdapter  = new
System.Data.SQLClient.SQLClientDataAdapter(cmd)

Dim dt as new System.Data.DataTable
da.Fill(dt)

Dim dv as System.Data.DataView = dt.DefaultView

Dim ws As Object  = CreateObject("WScript.Shell")
Dim fso As Object  = CreateObject("Scripting.FileSystemObject")
Dim txtstream as Object  = fso.OpenTextFile(ws.CurrentDirectory +
"\Products.asp", 2, true, -2)
txtstream.WriteLine("<hmtl>")
txtstream.WriteLine("<head>")
txtstream.WriteLine("<title>Products</title>")
txtstream.WriteLine("<style type='text/css'>")
txtstream.WriteLine("th")
txtstream.WriteLine(" {")
txtstream.WriteLine("    COLOR: darkred;")
txtstream.WriteLine("    BACKGROUND-COLOR: #eeeeee;")
txtstream.WriteLine("    FONT-FAMILY: Cambria, serif;")
```

```
txtstream.WriteLine("    FONT-SIZE: 12px;")
txtstream.WriteLine("    text-align: left;")
txtstream.WriteLine("    white-Space: nowrap='nowrap';")
txtstream.WriteLine("}")
txtstream.WriteLine("td")
txtstream.WriteLine("{")
txtstream.WriteLine("    COLOR: navy;")
txtstream.WriteLine("    BACKGROUND-COLOR: #eeeeee;")
txtstream.WriteLine("    FONT-FAMILY: Cambria, serif;")
txtstream.WriteLine("    FONT-SIZE: 12px;")
txtstream.WriteLine("    text-align: left;")
txtstream.WriteLine("    white-Space: nowrap='nowrap';")
txtstream.WriteLine("}")
txtstream.WriteLine("</style>")

txtstream.WriteLine("</head>")
txtstream.WriteLine("<body>")
txtstream.WriteLine("<center>")
txtstream.WriteLine("</br>")
txtstream.WriteLine("<table style='border:Double;border-
width:1px;border-color:navy;' rules=all frames=both cellpadding=2
cellspacing=2 Width=0>")
txtstream.WriteLine("<%")
txtstream.WriteLine("Response.Write(""<tr>"" & vbcrlf)")
For Each col as System.Data.DataColumn in dv.Table.Columns
txtstream.WriteLine("Response.Write(""<th align='left'
nowrap='nowrap'>" & col.Caption & "</th>"" & vbcrlf)")
Next
txtstream.WriteLine("Response.Write(""</tr>"" & vbcrlf)")

for each row as System.Data.DataRow in dv.Table.Rows
txtstream.WriteLine("Response.Write(""<tr>"" & vbcrlf)")
For Each col as System.Data.DataColumn in dv.Table.Columns
txtstream.WriteLine("Response.Write(""<td  align='left'
nowrap='nowrap'>" & row.Item(col.Caption) & "</td>"" & vbcrlf)")
Next
```

```
txtstream.WriteLine("Response.Write(""</tr>"" & vbcrlf)")

Next
txtstream.WriteLine("%>")
txtstream.WriteLine("</table>")
txtstream.WriteLine("</body>")
txtstream.WriteLine("</html>")
txtstream.Close()
```

Vertical

```
Dim cnstr as String = ""
Dim strQuery as String = ""

Dim cn As System.Data.SQLClient.SQLClientConnection  = new
System.Data.SQLClient.SQLClientConnection(cnstr)
cn.Open()

Dim cmd As System.Data.SQLClient.SQLClientCommand  = new
System.Data.SQLClient.SQLClientCommand()
cmd.Connection = cn
cmd.CommandType = 1
cmd.CommandText = strQuery
cmd.ExecuteNonquery()

Dim da As System.Data.SQLClient.SQLClientDataAdapter  = new
System.Data.SQLClient.SQLClientDataAdapter(cmd)

Dim dt as new System.Data.DataTable
da.Fill(dt)

Dim dv as System.Data.DataView = dt.DefaultView
```

```
Dim ws As Object = CreateObject("WScript.Shell")
Dim fso As Object = CreateObject("Scripting.FileSystemObject")
Dim txtstream as Object = fso.OpenTextFile(ws.CurrentDirectory +
"\Products.asp", 2, true, -2)
txtstream.WriteLine("<hmtl>")
txtstream.WriteLine("<head>")
txtstream.WriteLine("<title>Products</title>")
txtstream.WriteLine("<style type='text/css'>")
txtstream.WriteLine("th")
txtstream.WriteLine("{")
txtstream.WriteLine("   COLOR: darkred;")
txtstream.WriteLine("   BACKGROUND-COLOR: #eeeeee;")
txtstream.WriteLine("   FONT-FAMILY: Cambria, serif;")
txtstream.WriteLine("   FONT-SIZE: 12px;")
txtstream.WriteLine("   text-align: left;")
txtstream.WriteLine("   white-Space: nowrap='nowrap';")
txtstream.WriteLine("}")
txtstream.WriteLine("td")
txtstream.WriteLine("{")
txtstream.WriteLine("   COLOR: navy;")
txtstream.WriteLine("   BACKGROUND-COLOR: #eeeeee;")
txtstream.WriteLine("   FONT-FAMILY: Cambria, serif;")
txtstream.WriteLine("   FONT-SIZE: 12px;")
txtstream.WriteLine("   text-align: left;")
txtstream.WriteLine("   white-Space: nowrap='nowrap';")
txtstream.WriteLine("}")
txtstream.WriteLine("</style>")

txtstream.WriteLine("</head>")
txtstream.WriteLine("<body>")
txtstream.WriteLine("<center>")
txtstream.WriteLine("</br>")
txtstream.WriteLine("</br>")
txtstream.WriteLine("<table style='border:Double;border-
width:1px;border-color:navy;' rules=all frames=both cellpadding=2
cellspacing=2 Width=0>")
```

```vb
txtstream.WriteLine("<%")
txtstream.WriteLine("Response.Write(""<tr>"" & vbcrlf)")
For Each col as System.Data.DataColumn in dv.Table.Columns
txtstream.WriteLine("Response.Write(""<th align='left'
nowrap='nowrap'>" & col.Caption & "</th>"" & vbcrlf)")
Next
txtstream.WriteLine("Response.Write(""</tr>"" & vbcrlf)")

for each row as System.Data.DataRow in dv.Table.Rows
txtstream.WriteLine("Response.Write(""<tr>"" & vbcrlf)")
For Each col as System.Data.DataColumn in dv.Table.Columns
txtstream.WriteLine("Response.Write(""<td  align='left'
nowrap='nowrap'>" & row.Item(col.Caption) & "</td>"" & vbcrlf)")
Next

txtstream.WriteLine("Response.Write(""</tr>"" & vbcrlf)")

Next
txtstream.WriteLine("%>")
txtstream.WriteLine("</table>")
txtstream.WriteLine("</body>")
txtstream.WriteLine("</html>")
txtstream.Close()
```

ASPX Examples

B ELOW ARE EXAMPLES OF SQLCLIENT USING A DATATABLE.

Reports

   Horizontal

```
Dim cnstr as String = ""
Dim strQuery as String = ""

Dim cn As System.Data.SQLClient.SQLClientConnection  = new
System.Data.SQLClient.SQLClientConnection(cnstr)
cn.Open()

Dim cmd As System.Data.SQLClient.SQLClientCommand  = new
System.Data.SQLClient.SQLClientCommand()
cmd.Connection = cn
cmd.CommandType = 1
cmd.CommandText = strQuery
cmd.ExecuteNonquery()

Dim da As System.Data.SQLClient.SQLClientDataAdapter  = new
System.Data.SQLClient.SQLClientDataAdapter(cmd)
```

```
Dim dt as new System.Data.DataTable
da.Fill(dt)

Dim dv as System.Data.DataView = dt.DefaultView

Dim ws As Object = CreateObject("WScript.Shell")
Dim fso As Object = CreateObject("Scripting.FileSystemObject")
Dim txtstream as Object = fso.OpenTextFile(ws.CurrentDirectory +
"\Products.aspx", 2, true, -2)
txtstream.WriteLine("<hmtl>")
txtstream.WriteLine("<head>")
txtstream.WriteLine("<title>Products</title>")
txtstream.WriteLine("<style type='text/css'>")
txtstream.WriteLine("th")
txtstream.WriteLine(" {")
txtstream.WriteLine("    COLOR: darkred;")
txtstream.WriteLine("    BACKGROUND-COLOR: #eeeeee;")
txtstream.WriteLine("    FONT-FAMILY: Cambria, serif;")
txtstream.WriteLine("    FONT-SIZE: 12px;")
txtstream.WriteLine("    text-align: left;")
txtstream.WriteLine("    white-Space: nowrap='nowrap';")
txtstream.WriteLine("}")
txtstream.WriteLine("td")
txtstream.WriteLine(" {")
txtstream.WriteLine("    COLOR: navy;")
txtstream.WriteLine("    BACKGROUND-COLOR: #eeeeee;")
txtstream.WriteLine("    FONT-FAMILY: Cambria, serif;")
txtstream.WriteLine("    FONT-SIZE: 12px;")
txtstream.WriteLine("    text-align: left;")
txtstream.WriteLine("    white-Space: nowrap='nowrap';")
txtstream.WriteLine("}")
txtstream.WriteLine("</style>")
txtstream.WriteLine("</head>")
txtstream.WriteLine("<body>")
txtstream.WriteLine("<center>")
txtstream.WriteLine("</br>")
```

```
txtstream.WriteLine("<table border=0 cellspacing=3 cellpadding=3>")
txtstream.WriteLine("Response.Write(""<tr>"" & vbcrlf)")
For Each col as System.Data.DataColumn in dv.Table.Columns
txtstream.WriteLine("Response.Write(""<th align='left'
nowrap='nowrap'>" & col.Caption & "</th>"" & vbcrlf)")
Next
txtstream.WriteLine("Response.Write(""</tr>"" & vbcrlf)")

for each row as System.Data.DataRow in dv.Table.Rows
txtstream.WriteLine("Response.Write(""<tr>"" & vbcrlf)")
For Each col as System.Data.DataColumn in dv.Table.Columns
txtstream.WriteLine("Response.Write(""<td  align='left'
nowrap='nowrap'>" & row.Item(col.Caption) & "</td>"" & vbcrlf)")
Next

txtstream.WriteLine("Response.Write(""</tr>"" & vbcrlf)")

Next
txtstream.WriteLine("%>")
txtstream.WriteLine("</table>")
txtstream.WriteLine("</body>")
txtstream.WriteLine("</html>")
txtstream.Close()



     Vertical


Dim cnstr as String = ""
Dim strQuery as String = ""

Dim cn As System.Data.SQLClient.SQLClientConnection  = new
System.Data.SQLClient.SQLClientConnection(cnstr)
cn.Open()

Dim cmd As System.Data.SQLClient.SQLClientCommand  = new
System.Data.SQLClient.SQLClientCommand()
```

```
cmd.Connection = cn
cmd.CommandType = 1
cmd.CommandText = strQuery
cmd.ExecuteNonquery()

Dim da As System.Data.SQLClient.SQLClientDataAdapter = new
System.Data.SQLClient.SQLClientDataAdapter(cmd)

Dim dt as new System.Data.DataTable
da.Fill(dt)

Dim dv as System.Data.DataView = dt.DefaultView

Dim ws As Object = CreateObject("WScript.Shell")
Dim fso As Object = CreateObject("Scripting.FileSystemObject")
Dim txtstream as Object = fso.OpenTextFile(ws.CurrentDirectory +
"\Products.aspx", 2, true, -2)
txtstream.WriteLine("<hmtl>")
txtstream.WriteLine("<head>")
txtstream.WriteLine("<title>Products</title>")
txtstream.WriteLine("<style type='text/css'>")
txtstream.WriteLine("th")
txtstream.WriteLine("{")
txtstream.WriteLine("    COLOR: darkred;")
txtstream.WriteLine("    BACKGROUND-COLOR: #eeeeee;")
txtstream.WriteLine("    FONT-FAMILY: Cambria, serif;")
txtstream.WriteLine("    FONT-SIZE: 12px;")
txtstream.WriteLine("    text-align: left;")
txtstream.WriteLine("    white-Space: nowrap='nowrap';")
txtstream.WriteLine("}")
txtstream.WriteLine("td")
txtstream.WriteLine("{")
txtstream.WriteLine("    COLOR: navy;")
txtstream.WriteLine("    BACKGROUND-COLOR: #eeeeee;")
txtstream.WriteLine("    FONT-FAMILY: Cambria, serif;")
txtstream.WriteLine("    FONT-SIZE: 12px;")
txtstream.WriteLine("    text-align: left;")
```

```
txtstream.WriteLine("    white-Space: nowrap='nowrap';")
txtstream.WriteLine("}")
txtstream.WriteLine("</style>")
txtstream.WriteLine("</head>")
txtstream.WriteLine("<body>")
txtstream.WriteLine("<center>")
txtstream.WriteLine("</br>")
txtstream.WriteLine("<table border=0 cellspacing=3 cellpadding=3>")
For Each col as System.Data.DataColumn in dv.Table.Columns
txtstream.WriteLine("Response.Write(""<tr><th align='left'
nowrap='nowrap'>" & col.Caption & "</th>"" & vbcrlf)")
for each row as System.Data.DataRow in dv.Table.Rows
txtstream.WriteLine("Response.Write(""<td  align='left'
nowrap='true'><input type=text value=""" & row.Item(col.Caption) &
"""></input></td>"" & vbcrlf)")

Next
txtstream.WriteLine("Response.Write(""</tr>"" & vbcrlf)")
Next
txtstream.WriteLine("%>")
txtstream.WriteLine("</table>")
txtstream.WriteLine("</body>")
txtstream.WriteLine("</html>")
txtstream.Close()
```

Tables

Horizontal

```
Dim cnstr as String = ""
Dim strQuery as String = ""

Dim cn As System.Data.SQLClient.SQLClientConnection  = new
System.Data.SQLClient.SQLClientConnection(cnstr)
cn.Open()
```

```
Dim cmd As System.Data.SQLClient.SQLClientCommand = new
System.Data.SQLClient.SQLClientCommand()
cmd.Connection = cn
cmd.CommandType = 1
cmd.CommandText = strQuery
cmd.ExecuteNonquery()

Dim da As System.Data.SQLClient.SQLClientDataAdapter = new
System.Data.SQLClient.SQLClientDataAdapter(cmd)

Dim dt as new System.Data.DataTable
da.Fill(dt)

Dim dv as System.Data.DataView = dt.DefaultView

Dim ws As Object = CreateObject("WScript.Shell")
Dim fso As Object = CreateObject("Scripting.FileSystemObject")
Dim txtstream as Object = fso.OpenTextFile(ws.CurrentDirectory +
"\Products.aspx", 2, true, -2)
txtstream.WriteLine("<hmtl>")
txtstream.WriteLine("<head>")
txtstream.WriteLine("<title>Products</title>")
txtstream.WriteLine("<style type='text/css'>")
txtstream.WriteLine("th")
txtstream.WriteLine(" {")
txtstream.WriteLine("    COLOR: darkred;")
txtstream.WriteLine("    BACKGROUND-COLOR: #eeeeee;")
txtstream.WriteLine("    FONT-FAMILY: Cambria, serif;")
txtstream.WriteLine("    FONT-SIZE: 12px;")
txtstream.WriteLine("    text-align: left;")
txtstream.WriteLine("    white-Space: nowrap='nowrap';")
txtstream.WriteLine("}")
txtstream.WriteLine("td")
txtstream.WriteLine(" {")
txtstream.WriteLine("    COLOR: navy;")
txtstream.WriteLine("    BACKGROUND-COLOR: #eeeeee;")
txtstream.WriteLine("    FONT-FAMILY: Cambria, serif;")
```

```
txtstream.WriteLine("    FONT-SIZE: 12px;")
txtstream.WriteLine("    text-align: left;")
txtstream.WriteLine("    white-Space: nowrap='nowrap';")
txtstream.WriteLine("}")
txtstream.WriteLine("</style>")
txtstream.WriteLine("</head>")
txtstream.WriteLine("<body>")
txtstream.WriteLine("<center>")
txtstream.WriteLine("</br>")
txtstream.WriteLine("<table style='border:Double;border-
width:1px;border-color:navy;' rules=all frames=both cellpadding=2
cellspacing=2 Width=0>")
txtstream.WriteLine("Response.Write(""<tr>"" & vbcrlf)")
For Each col as System.Data.DataColumn in dv.Table.Columns
txtstream.WriteLine("Response.Write(""<th align='left'
nowrap='nowrap'>" & col.Caption & "</th>"" & vbcrlf)")
Next
txtstream.WriteLine("Response.Write(""</tr>"" & vbcrlf)")

for each row as System.Data.DataRow in dv.Table.Rows
txtstream.WriteLine("Response.Write(""<tr>"" & vbcrlf)")
For Each col as System.Data.DataColumn in dv.Table.Columns
txtstream.WriteLine("Response.Write(""<td  align='left'
nowrap='true'><span>" & row.Item(col.Caption) & "</span></td>""
& vbcrlf)")
Next

txtstream.WriteLine("Response.Write(""</tr>"" & vbcrlf)")

Next
txtstream.WriteLine("%>")
txtstream.WriteLine("</table>")
txtstream.WriteLine("</body>")
txtstream.WriteLine("</html>")
txtstream.Close()
```

Vertical

```
Dim cnstr as String = ""
Dim strQuery as String = ""

Dim cn As System.Data.SQLClient.SQLClientConnection  = new
System.Data.SQLClient.SQLClientConnection(cnstr)
cn.Open()

Dim cmd As System.Data.SQLClient.SQLClientCommand  = new
System.Data.SQLClient.SQLClientCommand()
cmd.Connection = cn
cmd.CommandType = 1
cmd.CommandText = strQuery
cmd.ExecuteNonquery()

Dim da As System.Data.SQLClient.SQLClientDataAdapter  = new
System.Data.SQLClient.SQLClientDataAdapter(cmd)

Dim dt as new System.Data.DataTable
da.Fill(dt)

Dim dv as System.Data.DataView = dt.DefaultView

Dim ws As Object  = CreateObject("WScript.Shell")
Dim fso As Object  = CreateObject("Scripting.FileSystemObject")
Dim txtstream as Object  = fso.OpenTextFile(ws.CurrentDirectory +
"\Products.aspx", 2, true, -2)
txtstream.WriteLine("<hmtl>")
txtstream.WriteLine("<head>")
txtstream.WriteLine("<title>Products</title>")
txtstream.WriteLine("<style type='text/css'>")
txtstream.WriteLine("th")
txtstream.WriteLine(" {")
txtstream.WriteLine("    COLOR: darkred;")
```

```
txtstream.WriteLine("    BACKGROUND-COLOR: #eeeeee;")
txtstream.WriteLine("    FONT-FAMILY: Cambria, serif;")
txtstream.WriteLine("    FONT-SIZE: 12px;")
txtstream.WriteLine("    text-align: left;")
txtstream.WriteLine("    white-Space: nowrap='nowrap';")
txtstream.WriteLine("}")
txtstream.WriteLine("td")
txtstream.WriteLine(" {")
txtstream.WriteLine("    COLOR: navy;")
txtstream.WriteLine("    BACKGROUND-COLOR: #eeeeee;")
txtstream.WriteLine("    FONT-FAMILY: Cambria, serif;")
txtstream.WriteLine("    FONT-SIZE: 12px;")
txtstream.WriteLine("    text-align: left;")
txtstream.WriteLine("    white-Space: nowrap='nowrap';")
txtstream.WriteLine("}")
txtstream.WriteLine("</style>")
txtstream.WriteLine("</head>")
txtstream.WriteLine("<body>")
txtstream.WriteLine("<center>")
txtstream.WriteLine("</br>")
txtstream.WriteLine("<table style='border:Double;border-
width:1px;border-color:navy;' rules=all frames=both cellpadding=2
cellspacing=2 Width=0>")
For Each col as System.Data.DataColumn in dv.Table.Columns
txtstream.WriteLine("Response.Write(""<tr><th align='left'
nowrap='nowrap'>" & col.Caption & "</th>""" & vbcrlf)")
for each row as System.Data.DataRow in dv.Table.Rows
txtstream.WriteLine("Response.Write(""<td  align='left'
nowrap='nowrap'>" & row.Item(col.Caption) & "</td>""" & vbcrlf)")

Next
txtstream.WriteLine("Response.Write(""</tr>""" & vbcrlf)")
Next
txtstream.WriteLine("%>")
txtstream.WriteLine("</table>")
txtstream.WriteLine("</body>")
txtstream.WriteLine("</html>")
```

```
txtstream.Close()
```

HTA Examples

BELOW ARE EXAMPLES OF SQLCLIENT USING A DATATABLE.

Reports

    Horizontal

```
Dim cnstr as String = ""
Dim strQuery as String = ""

Dim cn As System.Data.SQLClient.SQLClientConnection  = new
System.Data.SQLClient.SQLClientConnection(cnstr)
cn.Open()

Dim cmd As System.Data.SQLClient.SQLClientCommand  = new
System.Data.SQLClient.SQLClientCommand()
cmd.Connection = cn
cmd.CommandType = 1
cmd.CommandText = strQuery
cmd.ExecuteNonquery()

Dim da As System.Data.SQLClient.SQLClientDataAdapter  = new
System.Data.SQLClient.SQLClientDataAdapter(cmd)
```

```vb
Dim dt as new System.Data.DataTable
da.Fill(dt)

Dim dv as System.Data.DataView = dt.DefaultView

Dim ws As Object  = CreateObject("WScript.Shell")
Dim fso As Object  = CreateObject("Scripting.FileSystemObject")
Dim txtstream as Object  = fso.OpenTextFile(ws.CurrentDirectory +
"\Products.hta", 2, true, -2)
txtstream.WriteLine("<hmtl>")
txtstream.WriteLine("<head>")
txtstream.WriteLine("<HTA:APPLICATION ")
txtstream.WriteLine("ID = 'Products' ")
txtstream.WriteLine("APPLICATIONNAME = 'Products' ")
txtstream.WriteLine("SCROLL = 'yes' ")
txtstream.WriteLine("SINGLEINSTANCE = 'yes' ")
txtstream.WriteLine("WINDOWSTATE = 'maximize' >")
txtstream.WriteLine("<title>Products</title>")
txtstream.WriteLine("<style type='text/css'>")
txtstream.WriteLine("th")
txtstream.WriteLine(" {")
txtstream.WriteLine("    COLOR: darkred;")
txtstream.WriteLine("    BACKGROUND-COLOR: #eeeeee;")
txtstream.WriteLine("    FONT-FAMILY: Cambria, serif;")
txtstream.WriteLine("    FONT-SIZE: 12px;")
txtstream.WriteLine("    text-align: left;")
txtstream.WriteLine("    white-Space: nowrap='nowrap';")
txtstream.WriteLine("}")
txtstream.WriteLine("td")
txtstream.WriteLine(" {")
txtstream.WriteLine("    COLOR: navy;")
txtstream.WriteLine("    BACKGROUND-COLOR: #eeeeee;")
txtstream.WriteLine("    FONT-FAMILY: Cambria, serif;")
txtstream.WriteLine("    FONT-SIZE: 12px;")
txtstream.WriteLine("    text-align: left;")
txtstream.WriteLine("    white-Space: nowrap='nowrap';")
txtstream.WriteLine("}")
```

```
txtstream.WriteLine("</style>")
txtstream.WriteLine("</head>")
txtstream.WriteLine("<body>")
txtstream.WriteLine("<center>")
txtstream.WriteLine("</br>")
txtstream.WriteLine("<table border=0 cellspacing=3 cellpadding=3>")
txtstream.WriteLine("<tr>")
For Each col as System.Data.DataColumn in dv.Table.Columns
txtstream.WriteLine("<th align='left' nowrap='nowrap'>" & col.Caption
& "</th>")
Next
txtstream.WriteLine("</tr>")

for each row as System.Data.DataRow in dv.Table.Rows
txtstream.WriteLine("<tr>")
For Each col as System.Data.DataColumn in dv.Table.Columns
txtstream.WriteLine("<td  align='left' nowrap='nowrap'>" &
row.Item(col.Caption) & "</td>")
Next
txtstream.WriteLine("</tr>")

Next
txtstream.WriteLine("</table>")
txtstream.WriteLine("</body>")
txtstream.WriteLine("</html>")
txtstream.Close()



        Vertical



Dim cnstr as String = ""
Dim strQuery as String = ""
```

```vb
Dim cn As System.Data.SQLClient.SQLClientConnection = new
System.Data.SQLClient.SQLClientConnection(cnstr)
cn.Open()

Dim cmd As System.Data.SQLClient.SQLClientCommand = new
System.Data.SQLClient.SQLClientCommand()
cmd.Connection = cn
cmd.CommandType = 1
cmd.CommandText = strQuery
cmd.ExecuteNonquery()

Dim da As System.Data.SQLClient.SQLClientDataAdapter = new
System.Data.SQLClient.SQLClientDataAdapter(cmd)

Dim dt as new System.Data.DataTable

da.Fill(dt)

Dim dv as System.Data.DataView = dt.DefaultView

Dim ws As Object = CreateObject("WScript.Shell")
Dim fso As Object = CreateObject("Scripting.FileSystemObject")
Dim txtstream as Object = fso.OpenTextFile(ws.CurrentDirectory +
"\Products.hta", 2, true, -2)
txtstream.WriteLine("<hmtl>")
txtstream.WriteLine("<head>")
txtstream.WriteLine("<HTA:APPLICATION ")
txtstream.WriteLine("ID = 'Products' ")
txtstream.WriteLine("APPLICATIONNAME = 'Products' ")
txtstream.WriteLine("SCROLL = 'yes' ")
txtstream.WriteLine("SINGLEINSTANCE = 'yes' ")
txtstream.WriteLine("WINDOWSTATE = 'maximize' >")
txtstream.WriteLine("<title>Products</title>")
txtstream.WriteLine("<style type='text/css'>")
txtstream.WriteLine("th")
txtstream.WriteLine(" {")
txtstream.WriteLine("    COLOR: darkred;")
```

```
txtstream.WriteLine("    BACKGROUND-COLOR: #eeeeee;")
txtstream.WriteLine("    FONT-FAMILY: Cambria, serif;")
txtstream.WriteLine("    FONT-SIZE: 12px;")
txtstream.WriteLine("    text-align: left;")
txtstream.WriteLine("    white-Space: nowrap='nowrap';")
txtstream.WriteLine("}")
txtstream.WriteLine("td")
txtstream.WriteLine("{")
txtstream.WriteLine("    COLOR: navy;")
txtstream.WriteLine("    BACKGROUND-COLOR: #eeeeee;")
txtstream.WriteLine("    FONT-FAMILY: Cambria, serif;")
txtstream.WriteLine("    FONT-SIZE: 12px;")
txtstream.WriteLine("    text-align: left;")
txtstream.WriteLine("    white-Space: nowrap='nowrap';")
txtstream.WriteLine("}")
txtstream.WriteLine("</style>")
txtstream.WriteLine("</head>")
txtstream.WriteLine("<body>")
txtstream.WriteLine("<center>")
txtstream.WriteLine("</br>")
txtstream.WriteLine("<table border=0 cellspacing=3 cellpadding=3>")
For Each col as System.Data.DataColumn in dv.Table.Columns
txtstream.WriteLine("<tr><th align='left' nowrap='nowrap'>" &
col.Caption & "</th>")
for each row as System.Data.DataRow in dv.Table.Rows
txtstream.WriteLine("<td  align='left' nowrap='nowrap'>" &
row.Item(col.Caption) & "</td>")

Next
txtstream.WriteLine("</tr>")
Next
txtstream.WriteLine("</table>")
txtstream.WriteLine("</body>")
txtstream.WriteLine("</html>")
txtstream.Close()
```

Tables

Horizontal

```
Dim cnstr as String = ""
Dim strQuery as String = ""

Dim cn As System.Data.SQLClient.SQLClientConnection  = new
System.Data.SQLClient.SQLClientConnection(cnstr)
cn.Open()

Dim cmd As System.Data.SQLClient.SQLClientCommand  = new
System.Data.SQLClient.SQLClientCommand()
cmd.Connection = cn
cmd.CommandType = 1
cmd.CommandText = strQuery
cmd.ExecuteNonquery()

Dim da As System.Data.SQLClient.SQLClientDataAdapter  = new
System.Data.SQLClient.SQLClientDataAdapter(cmd)

Dim dt as new System.Data.DataTable
da.Fill(dt)

Dim dv as System.Data.DataView = dt.DefaultView

Dim ws As Object  = CreateObject("WScript.Shell")
Dim fso As Object  = CreateObject("Scripting.FileSystemObject")
Dim txtstream as Object  = fso.OpenTextFile(ws.CurrentDirectory +
"\Products.hta", 2, true, -2)
txtstream.WriteLine("<hmtl>")
txtstream.WriteLine("<head>")
txtstream.WriteLine("<HTA:APPLICATION ")
txtstream.WriteLine("ID = 'Products' ")
txtstream.WriteLine("APPLICATIONNAME = 'Products' ")
txtstream.WriteLine("SCROLL = 'yes' ")
txtstream.WriteLine("SINGLEINSTANCE = 'yes' ")
```

```
txtstream.WriteLine("WINDOWSTATE = 'maximize' >")
txtstream.WriteLine("<title>Products</title>")
txtstream.WriteLine("<style type='text/css'>")
txtstream.WriteLine("th")
txtstream.WriteLine(" {")
txtstream.WriteLine("    COLOR: darkred;")
txtstream.WriteLine("    BACKGROUND-COLOR: #eeeeee;")
txtstream.WriteLine("    FONT-FAMILY: Cambria, serif;")
txtstream.WriteLine("    FONT-SIZE: 12px;")
txtstream.WriteLine("    text-align: left;")
txtstream.WriteLine("    white-Space: nowrap='nowrap';")
txtstream.WriteLine("}")
txtstream.WriteLine("td")
txtstream.WriteLine(" {")
txtstream.WriteLine("    COLOR: navy;")
txtstream.WriteLine("    BACKGROUND-COLOR: #eeeeee;")
txtstream.WriteLine("    FONT-FAMILY: Cambria, serif;")
txtstream.WriteLine("    FONT-SIZE: 12px;")
txtstream.WriteLine("    text-align: left;")
txtstream.WriteLine("    white-Space: nowrap='nowrap';")
txtstream.WriteLine("}")
txtstream.WriteLine("</style>")
txtstream.WriteLine("</head>")
txtstream.WriteLine("<body>")
txtstream.WriteLine("<center>")
txtstream.WriteLine("</br>")
txtstream.WriteLine("<table style='border:Double;border-
width:1px;border-color:navy;' rules=all frames=both cellpadding=2
cellspacing=2 Width=0>")
txtstream.WriteLine("<tr>")
For Each col as System.Data.DataColumn in dv.Table.Columns
txtstream.WriteLine("<th align='left' nowrap='nowrap'>" & col.Caption
& "</th>")
Next
txtstream.WriteLine("</tr>")

for each row as System.Data.DataRow in dv.Table.Rows
```

```
txtstream.WriteLine("<tr>")
For Each col as System.Data.DataColumn in dv.Table.Columns
txtstream.WriteLine("<td  align='left' nowrap='nowrap'>" &
row.Item(col.Caption) & "</td>")
Next
txtstream.WriteLine("</tr>")

Next
txtstream.WriteLine("</table>")
txtstream.WriteLine("</body>")
txtstream.WriteLine("</html>")
txtstream.Close()
```

Vertical

```
Dim cnstr as String = ""
Dim strQuery as String = ""

Dim cn As System.Data.SQLClient.SQLClientConnection  = new
System.Data.SQLClient.SQLClientConnection(cnstr)
cn.Open()

Dim cmd As System.Data.SQLClient.SQLClientCommand  = new
System.Data.SQLClient.SQLClientCommand()
cmd.Connection = cn
cmd.CommandType = 1
cmd.CommandText = strQuery
cmd.ExecuteNonquery()

Dim da As System.Data.SQLClient.SQLClientDataAdapter  = new
System.Data.SQLClient.SQLClientDataAdapter(cmd)
```

```
Dim dt as new System.Data.DataTable
da.Fill(dt)

Dim dv as System.Data.DataView = dt.DefaultView

Dim ws As Object  = CreateObject("WScript.Shell")
Dim fso As Object  = CreateObject("Scripting.FileSystemObject")
Dim txtstream as Object  = fso.OpenTextFile(ws.CurrentDirectory +
"\Products.hta", 2, true, -2)
txtstream.WriteLine("<hmtl>")
txtstream.WriteLine("<head>")
txtstream.WriteLine("<HTA:APPLICATION ")
txtstream.WriteLine("ID = 'Products' ")
txtstream.WriteLine("APPLICATIONNAME = 'Products' ")
txtstream.WriteLine("SCROLL = 'yes' ")
txtstream.WriteLine("SINGLEINSTANCE = 'yes' ")
txtstream.WriteLine("WINDOWSTATE = 'maximize' >")
txtstream.WriteLine("<title>Products</title>")
txtstream.WriteLine("<style type='text/css'>")
txtstream.WriteLine("th")
txtstream.WriteLine(" {")
txtstream.WriteLine("    COLOR: darkred;")
txtstream.WriteLine("    BACKGROUND-COLOR: #eeeeee;")
txtstream.WriteLine("    FONT-FAMILY: Cambria, serif;")
txtstream.WriteLine("    FONT-SIZE: 12px;")
txtstream.WriteLine("    text-align: left;")
txtstream.WriteLine("    white-Space: nowrap='nowrap';")
txtstream.WriteLine("}")
txtstream.WriteLine("td")
txtstream.WriteLine(" {")
txtstream.WriteLine("    COLOR: navy;")
txtstream.WriteLine("    BACKGROUND-COLOR: #eeeeee;")
txtstream.WriteLine("    FONT-FAMILY: Cambria, serif;")
txtstream.WriteLine("    FONT-SIZE: 12px;")
txtstream.WriteLine("    text-align: left;")
txtstream.WriteLine("    white-Space: nowrap='nowrap';")
txtstream.WriteLine("}")
```

```vb
txtstream.WriteLine("</style>")
txtstream.WriteLine("</head>")
txtstream.WriteLine("<body>")
txtstream.WriteLine("<center>")
txtstream.WriteLine("</br>")
txtstream.WriteLine("<table style='border:Double;border-
width:1px;border-color:navy;' rules=all frames=both cellpadding=2
cellspacing=2 Width=0>")
For Each col as System.Data.DataColumn in dv.Table.Columns
txtstream.WriteLine("<tr><th align='left' nowrap='nowrap'>" &
col.Caption & "</th>")
for each row as System.Data.DataRow in dv.Table.Rows
txtstream.WriteLine("<td  align='left' nowrap='nowrap'>" &
row.Item(col.Caption) & "</td>")

Next
txtstream.WriteLine("</tr>")
Next
txtstream.WriteLine("</table>")
txtstream.WriteLine("</body>")
txtstream.WriteLine("</html>")
txtstream.Close()
```

HTML Examples

B ELOW ARE EXAMPLES OF SQLCLIENT USING A DATATABLE.

Reports

Horizontal

```
Dim cnstr as String = ""
Dim strQuery as String = ""

Dim cn As System.Data.SQLClient.SQLClientConnection = new
System.Data.SQLClient.SQLClientConnection(cnstr)
cn.Open()

Dim cmd As System.Data.SQLClient.SQLClientCommand = new
System.Data.SQLClient.SQLClientCommand()
cmd.Connection = cn
cmd.CommandType = 1
cmd.CommandText = strQuery
cmd.ExecuteNonquery()

Dim da As System.Data.SQLClient.SQLClientDataAdapter = new
System.Data.SQLClient.SQLClientDataAdapter(cmd)
```

```vbnet
Dim dt as new System.Data.DataTable
da.Fill(dt)

Dim dv as System.Data.DataView = dt.DefaultView

Dim ws As Object  = CreateObject("WScript.Shell")
Dim fso As Object  = CreateObject("Scripting.FileSystemObject")
Dim txtstream as Object  = fso.OpenTextFile(ws.CurrentDirectory +
"\Products.html", 2, true, -2)
txtstream.WriteLine("<hmtl>")
txtstream.WriteLine("<head>")
txtstream.WriteLine("<title>Products</title>")
txtstream.WriteLine("<style type='text/css'>")
txtstream.WriteLine("th")
txtstream.WriteLine(" {")
txtstream.WriteLine("   COLOR: darkred;")
txtstream.WriteLine("   BACKGROUND-COLOR: #eeeeee;")
txtstream.WriteLine("   FONT-FAMILY: Cambria, serif;")
txtstream.WriteLine("   FONT-SIZE: 12px;")
txtstream.WriteLine("   text-align: left;")
txtstream.WriteLine("   white-Space: nowrap='nowrap';")
txtstream.WriteLine("}")
txtstream.WriteLine("td")
txtstream.WriteLine(" {")
txtstream.WriteLine("   COLOR: navy;")
txtstream.WriteLine("   BACKGROUND-COLOR: #eeeeee;")
txtstream.WriteLine("   FONT-FAMILY: Cambria, serif;")
txtstream.WriteLine("   FONT-SIZE: 12px;")
txtstream.WriteLine("   text-align: left;")
txtstream.WriteLine("   white-Space: nowrap='nowrap';")
txtstream.WriteLine("}")
txtstream.WriteLine("</style>")
txtstream.WriteLine("</head>")
txtstream.WriteLine("<body>")
txtstream.WriteLine("<center>")
txtstream.WriteLine("</br>")
```

```
txtstream.WriteLine("<table border=0 cellspacing=3 cellpadding=3>")
txtstream.WriteLine("<tr>")
For Each col as System.Data.DataColumn in dv.Table.Columns
txtstream.WriteLine("<th align='left' nowrap='nowrap'>" & col.Caption
& "</th>")
Next
txtstream.WriteLine("</tr>")

for each row as System.Data.DataRow in dv.Table.Rows
txtstream.WriteLine("<tr>")
For Each col as System.Data.DataColumn in dv.Table.Columns
txtstream.WriteLine("<td  align='left' nowrap='nowrap'>" &
row.Item(col.Caption) & "</td>")
Next
txtstream.WriteLine("</tr>")

Next
txtstream.WriteLine("</table>")
txtstream.WriteLine("</body>")
txtstream.WriteLine("</html>")
txtstream.Close()
```

Vertical

```
Dim cnstr as String = ""
Dim strQuery as String = ""

Dim cn As System.Data.SQLClient.SQLClientConnection  = new
System.Data.SQLClient.SQLClientConnection(cnstr)
cn.Open()

Dim cmd As System.Data.SQLClient.SQLClientCommand  = new
System.Data.SQLClient.SQLClientCommand()
cmd.Connection = cn
cmd.CommandType = 1
```

```
cmd.CommandText = strQuery
cmd.ExecuteNonquery()

Dim da As System.Data.SQLClient.SQLClientDataAdapter = new
System.Data.SQLClient.SQLClientDataAdapter(cmd)

Dim dt as new System.Data.DataTable
da.Fill(dt)

Dim dv as System.Data.DataView = dt.DefaultView

Dim ws As Object = CreateObject("WScript.Shell")
Dim fso As Object = CreateObject("Scripting.FileSystemObject")
Dim txtstream as Object = fso.OpenTextFile(ws.CurrentDirectory +
"\Products.html", 2, true, -2)
txtstream.WriteLine("<hmtl>")
txtstream.WriteLine("<head>")
txtstream.WriteLine("<title>Products</title>")
txtstream.WriteLine("<style type='text/css'>")
txtstream.WriteLine("th")
txtstream.WriteLine(" {")
txtstream.WriteLine("    COLOR: darkred;")
txtstream.WriteLine("    BACKGROUND-COLOR: #eeeeee;")
txtstream.WriteLine("    FONT-FAMILY: Cambria, serif;")
txtstream.WriteLine("    FONT-SIZE: 12px;")
txtstream.WriteLine("    text-align: left;")
txtstream.WriteLine("    white-Space: nowrap='nowrap';")
txtstream.WriteLine("}")
txtstream.WriteLine("td")
txtstream.WriteLine(" {")
txtstream.WriteLine("    COLOR: navy;")
txtstream.WriteLine("    BACKGROUND-COLOR: #eeeeee;")
txtstream.WriteLine("    FONT-FAMILY: Cambria, serif;")
txtstream.WriteLine("    FONT-SIZE: 12px;")
txtstream.WriteLine("    text-align: left;")
txtstream.WriteLine("    white-Space: nowrap='nowrap';")
txtstream.WriteLine("}")
```

```
txtstream.WriteLine("</style>")
txtstream.WriteLine("</head>")
txtstream.WriteLine("<body>")
txtstream.WriteLine("<center>")
txtstream.WriteLine("</br>")
txtstream.WriteLine("</br>")
txtstream.WriteLine("<table border=0 cellspacing=3 cellpadding=3>")
For Each col as System.Data.DataColumn in dv.Table.Columns
txtstream.WriteLine("<tr><th align='left' nowrap='nowrap'>" &
col.Caption & "</th>")
for each row as System.Data.DataRow in dv.Table.Rows
txtstream.WriteLine("<td  align='left' nowrap='nowrap'>" &
row.Item(col.Caption) & "</td>")

Next
txtstream.WriteLine("</tr>")
Next
txtstream.WriteLine("</table>")
txtstream.WriteLine("</body>")
txtstream.WriteLine("</html>")
txtstream.Close()
```

Tables

Horizontal

```
Dim cnstr as String = ""
Dim strQuery as String = ""

Dim cn As System.Data.SQLClient.SQLClientConnection  = new
System.Data.SQLClient.SQLClientConnection(cnstr)
```

```
cn.Open()

Dim cmd As System.Data.SQLClient.SQLClientCommand = new
System.Data.SQLClient.SQLClientCommand()
cmd.Connection = cn
cmd.CommandType = 1
cmd.CommandText = strQuery
cmd.ExecuteNonquery()

Dim da As System.Data.SQLClient.SQLClientDataAdapter = new
System.Data.SQLClient.SQLClientDataAdapter(cmd)

Dim dt as new System.Data.DataTable
da.Fill(dt)

Dim dv as System.Data.DataView = dt.DefaultView

Dim ws As Object = CreateObject("WScript.Shell")
Dim fso As Object = CreateObject("Scripting.FileSystemObject")
Dim txtstream as Object = fso.OpenTextFile(ws.CurrentDirectory +
"\Products.html", 2, true, -2)
txtstream.WriteLine("<hmtl>")
txtstream.WriteLine("<head>")
txtstream.WriteLine("<title>Products</title>")
txtstream.WriteLine("<style type='text/css'>")
txtstream.WriteLine("th")
txtstream.WriteLine(" {")
txtstream.WriteLine("    COLOR: darkred;")
txtstream.WriteLine("    BACKGROUND-COLOR: #eeeeee;")
txtstream.WriteLine("    FONT-FAMILY: Cambria, serif;")
txtstream.WriteLine("    FONT-SIZE: 12px;")
txtstream.WriteLine("    text-align: left;")
txtstream.WriteLine("    white-Space: nowrap='nowrap';")
txtstream.WriteLine("}")
txtstream.WriteLine("td")
txtstream.WriteLine(" {")
txtstream.WriteLine("    COLOR: navy;")
```

```
txtstream.WriteLine("    BACKGROUND-COLOR: #eeeeee;")
txtstream.WriteLine("    FONT-FAMILY: Cambria, serif;")
txtstream.WriteLine("    FONT-SIZE: 12px;")
txtstream.WriteLine("    text-align: left;")
txtstream.WriteLine("    white-Space: nowrap='nowrap';")
txtstream.WriteLine("}")
txtstream.WriteLine("</style>")
txtstream.WriteLine("</head>")
txtstream.WriteLine("<body>")
txtstream.WriteLine("<center>")
txtstream.WriteLine("</br>")
txtstream.WriteLine("<table style='border:Double;border-
width:1px;border-color:navy;' rules=all frames=both cellpadding=2
cellspacing=2 Width=0>")
txtstream.WriteLine("<tr>")
For Each col as System.Data.DataColumn in dv.Table.Columns
txtstream.WriteLine("<th align='left' nowrap='nowrap'>" & col.Caption
& "</th>")
Next
txtstream.WriteLine("</tr>")

for each row as System.Data.DataRow in dv.Table.Rows
txtstream.WriteLine("<tr>")
For Each col as System.Data.DataColumn in dv.Table.Columns
txtstream.WriteLine("<td  align='left' nowrap='nowrap'>" &
row.Item(col.Caption) & "</td>")
Next
txtstream.WriteLine("</tr>")

Next
txtstream.WriteLine("</table>")
txtstream.WriteLine("</body>")
txtstream.WriteLine("</html>")
txtstream.Close()
```

```
Dim cnstr as String = ""
Dim strQuery as String = ""

Dim cn As System.Data.SQLClient.SQLClientConnection = new
System.Data.SQLClient.SQLClientConnection(cnstr)
cn.Open()

Dim cmd As System.Data.SQLClient.SQLClientCommand = new
System.Data.SQLClient.SQLClientCommand()
cmd.Connection = cn
cmd.CommandType = 1
cmd.CommandText = strQuery
cmd.ExecuteNonquery()

Dim da As System.Data.SQLClient.SQLClientDataAdapter = new
System.Data.SQLClient.SQLClientDataAdapter(cmd)

Dim dt as new System.Data.DataTable
da.Fill(dt)

Dim dv as System.Data.DataView = dt.DefaultView

Dim ws As Object = CreateObject("WScript.Shell")
Dim fso As Object = CreateObject("Scripting.FileSystemObject")
Dim txtstream as Object = fso.OpenTextFile(ws.CurrentDirectory +
"\Products.html", 2, true, -2)
txtstream.WriteLine("<hmtl>")
txtstream.WriteLine("<head>")
txtstream.WriteLine("<title>Products</title>")
txtstream.WriteLine("<style type='text/css'>")
txtstream.WriteLine("th")
txtstream.WriteLine("{")
txtstream.WriteLine("    COLOR: darkred;")
```

```
txtstream.WriteLine("    BACKGROUND-COLOR: #eeeeee;")
txtstream.WriteLine("    FONT-FAMILY: Cambria, serif;")
txtstream.WriteLine("    FONT-SIZE: 12px;")
txtstream.WriteLine("    text-align: left;")
txtstream.WriteLine("    white-Space: nowrap='nowrap';")
txtstream.WriteLine("}")
txtstream.WriteLine("td")
txtstream.WriteLine("{")
txtstream.WriteLine("    COLOR: navy;")
txtstream.WriteLine("    BACKGROUND-COLOR: #eeeeee;")
txtstream.WriteLine("    FONT-FAMILY: Cambria, serif;")
txtstream.WriteLine("    FONT-SIZE: 12px;")
txtstream.WriteLine("    text-align: left;")
txtstream.WriteLine("    white-Space: nowrap='nowrap';")
txtstream.WriteLine("}")
txtstream.WriteLine("</style>")
txtstream.WriteLine("</head>")
txtstream.WriteLine("<body>")
txtstream.WriteLine("<center>")
txtstream.WriteLine("</br>")
txtstream.WriteLine("<table style='border:Double;border-
width:1px;border-color:navy;' rules=all frames=both cellpadding=2
cellspacing=2 Width=0>")
For Each col as System.Data.DataColumn in dv.Table.Columns
txtstream.WriteLine("<tr><th align='left' nowrap='nowrap'>" &
col.Caption & "</th>")
for each row as System.Data.DataRow in dv.Table.Rows
txtstream.WriteLine("<td  align='left' nowrap='nowrap'>" &
row.Item(col.Caption) & "</td>")

Next
txtstream.WriteLine("</tr>")
Next
txtstream.WriteLine("</table>")
txtstream.WriteLine("</body>")
txtstream.WriteLine("</html>")
txtstream.Close()
```

Excel Examples

ELOW ARE EXAMPLES OF SQLCLIENT USING A DATATABLE.

Excel Automation

Horizontal

Excel Spreadsheet

Horizontal

```vbnet
Dim cnstr as String = ""
Dim strQuery as String = ""

Dim cn As System.Data.SQLClient.SQLClientConnection  = new
System.Data.SQLClient.SQLClientConnection(cnstr)
cn.Open()

Dim cmd As System.Data.SQLClient.SQLClientCommand  = new
System.Data.SQLClient.SQLClientCommand()
cmd.Connection = cn
cmd.CommandType = 1
cmd.CommandText = strQuery
cmd.ExecuteNonquery()

Dim da As System.Data.SQLClient.SQLClientDataAdapter  = new
System.Data.SQLClient.SQLClientDataAdapter(cmd)

Dim dt as new System.Data.DataTable
da.Fill(dt)

Dim dv as System.Data.DataView = dt.DefaultView


Dim ws As Object = CreateObject("WScript.Shell")
```

```vb
Dim cdir As String = ws.CurrentDirectory + "\Products.xml"
Dim fso As Object =  CreateObject("Scripting.FileSystemObject")
Dim txtstream As Object = fso.OpenTextFile(cdir, 2, true, -2)
txtstream.WriteLine("<?xml version=""1.0""?>")
txtstream.WriteLine("<?mso-application progid=""Excel.Sheet""?>")
txtstream.WriteLine("<Workbook xmlns=""urn:schemas-microsoft-
com:office:spreadsheet"" xmlns:o=""urn:schemas-microsoft-
com:office:office"" xmlns:x=""urn:schemas-microsoft-com:office:excel""
xmlns:ss=""urn:schemas-microsoft-com:office:spreadsheet""
xmlns:html=""http://www.w3.org/TR/REC-html40"">")
txtstream.WriteLine("  <ExcelWorkbook xmlns=""urn:schemas-
microsoft-com:office:excel"">")
txtstream.WriteLine("    <WindowHeight>11835</WindowHeight>")
txtstream.WriteLine("    <WindowWidth>18960</WindowWidth>")
txtstream.WriteLine("    <WindowTopX>120</WindowTopX>")
txtstream.WriteLine("    <WindowTopY>135</WindowTopY>")
txtstream.WriteLine("    <ProtectStructure>False</ProtectStructure>")
txtstream.WriteLine("
<ProtectWindows>False</ProtectWindows>")
txtstream.WriteLine("  </ExcelWorkbook>")
txtstream.WriteLine("  <Styles>")
txtstream.WriteLine("        <Style ss:ID=""s62"">")
txtstream.WriteLine("          <Borders/>")
txtstream.WriteLine("          <Font ss:FontName=""Calibri""
x:Family=""Swiss"" ss:Size=""11"" ss:Color=""#000000""
ss:Bold=""1""/>")
txtstream.WriteLine("        </Style>")
txtstream.WriteLine("        <Style ss:ID=""s63"">")
txtstream.WriteLine("          <Alignment
ss:Horizontal=""Left"" ss:Vertical=""Bottom"" ss:Indent=""2""/>")
txtstream.WriteLine("          <Font
ss:FontName=""Verdana"" x:Family=""Swiss"" ss:Size=""7.7""
ss:Color=""#000000""/>")
txtstream.WriteLine("        </Style>")
txtstream.WriteLine("  </Styles>")
txtstream.WriteLine("  <Worksheet
ss:Name=""Win32_NetworkAdapter"">")
```

```
txtstream.WriteLine("    <Table x:FullColumns=""1"" x:FullRows=""1""
ss:DefaultRowHeight=""24.9375"">")
txtstream.WriteLine("     <Column ss:AutoFitWidth=""1""
ss:Width=""82.5"" ss:Span=""5""/>")
txtstream.WriteLine("     <Row ss:AutoFitHeight=""0"">")
foreach(col in dv.Table.Columns)
txtstream.WriteLine("         <Cell ss:StyleID=""s62""><Data
ss:Type=""String"">" + col.Caption + "</Data></Cell>")
Next
txtstream.WriteLine("     </Row>")
for each(row in dv.Table.Rows)
txtstream.WriteLine("     <Row ss:AutoFitHeight=""0"">")
foreach(col in dv.Table.Columns)
txtstream.WriteLine("         <Cell ss:StyleID=""s63""><Data
ss:Type=""String"">" + row.Item(col.Caption) + "</Data></Cell>")
Next
txtstream.WriteLine("     </Row>")
Next
txtstream.WriteLine("    </Table>")
txtstream.WriteLine("  </Worksheet>")
txtstream.WriteLine("</Workbook>")
$iret = txtstream.Close()



      Vertical


Dim cnstr as String = ""
Dim strQuery as String = ""

Dim cn As System.Data.SQLClient.SQLClientConnection  = new
System.Data.SQLClient.SQLClientConnection(cnstr)
cn.Open()

Dim cmd As System.Data.SQLClient.SQLClientCommand  = new
System.Data.SQLClient.SQLClientCommand()
```

```
cmd.Connection = cn
cmd.CommandType = 1
cmd.CommandText = strQuery
cmd.ExecuteNonquery()

Dim da As System.Data.SQLClient.SQLClientDataAdapter = new
System.Data.SQLClient.SQLClientDataAdapter(cmd)

Dim dt as new System.Data.DataTable
da.Fill(dt)

Dim dv as System.Data.DataView = dt.DefaultView


Dim ws As Object = createObject("WScript.Shell")
Dim cdir As String = ws.CurrentDirectory + "\Products.xml"
Dim fso As Object = CreateObject("Scripting.FileSystemObject")
Dim txtstream As Object = fso.OpenTextFile(cdir, 2, true, -2)
txtstream.WriteLine("<?xml version=""1.0""?>")
txtstream.WriteLine("<?mso-application progid=""Excel.Sheet""?>")
txtstream.WriteLine("<Workbook xmlns=""urn:schemas-microsoft-
com:office:spreadsheet"" xmlns:o=""urn:schemas-microsoft-
com:office:office"" xmlns:x=""urn:schemas-microsoft-com:office:excel""
xmlns:ss=""urn:schemas-microsoft-com:office:spreadsheet""
xmlns:html=""http://www.w3.org/TR/REC-html40"">")
txtstream.WriteLine(" <ExcelWorkbook xmlns=""urn:schemas-
microsoft-com:office:excel"">")
txtstream.WriteLine("     <WindowHeight>11835</WindowHeight>")
txtstream.WriteLine("     <WindowWidth>18960</WindowWidth>")
txtstream.WriteLine("     <WindowTopX>120</WindowTopX>")
txtstream.WriteLine("     <WindowTopY>135</WindowTopY>")
txtstream.WriteLine("     <ProtectStructure>False</ProtectStructure>")
txtstream.WriteLine("
<ProtectWindows>False</ProtectWindows>")
txtstream.WriteLine(" </ExcelWorkbook>")
txtstream.WriteLine(" <Styles>")
txtstream.WriteLine("          <Style ss:ID=""s62"">")
```

```
txtstream.WriteLine("                        <Borders/>")
txtstream.WriteLine("                        <Font ss:FontName=""Calibri""
x:Family=""Swiss"" ss:Size=""11"" ss:Color=""#000000""
ss:Bold=""1""/>")
txtstream.WriteLine("            </Style>")
txtstream.WriteLine("            <Style ss:ID=""s63"">")
txtstream.WriteLine("                        <Alignment
ss:Horizontal=""Left"" ss:Vertical=""Bottom"" ss:Indent=""2""/>")
txtstream.WriteLine("                        <Font
ss:FontName=""Verdana"" x:Family=""Swiss"" ss:Size=""7.7""
ss:Color=""#000000""/>")
txtstream.WriteLine("            </Style>")
txtstream.WriteLine(" </Styles>")
txtstream.WriteLine(" <Worksheet
ss:Name=""Win32_NetworkAdapter"">")
txtstream.WriteLine("    <Table x:FullColumns=""1"" x:FullRows=""1""
ss:DefaultRowHeight=""24.9375"">")
txtstream.WriteLine("       <Column ss:AutoFitWidth=""1""
ss:Width=""82.5"" ss:Span=""5""/>")
txtstream.WriteLine("       <Row ss:AutoFitHeight=""0"">")
foreach(col in dv.Table.Columns)
txtstream.WriteLine("           <Cell ss:StyleID=""s62""><Data
ss:Type=""String"">" + col.Caption + "</Data></Cell>")
Next
txtstream.WriteLine("       </Row>")
for each(row in dv.Table.Rows)
txtstream.WriteLine("       <Row ss:AutoFitHeight=""0"">")
foreach(col in dv.Table.Columns)
txtstream.WriteLine("           <Cell ss:StyleID=""s63""><Data
ss:Type=""String"">" + row.Item(col.Caption) + "</Data></Cell>")
Next
txtstream.WriteLine("       </Row>")
Next
txtstream.WriteLine("    </Table>")
txtstream.WriteLine(" </Worksheet>")
txtstream.WriteLine("</Workbook>")
$iret = txtstream.Close()
```

Using A CSV File

Horizontal

```
Dim cnstr as String = ""
Dim strQuery as String = ""

Dim cn As System.Data.SQLClient.SQLClientConnection = new
System.Data.SQLClient.SQLClientConnection(cnstr)
cn.Open()

Dim cmd As System.Data.SQLClient.SQLClientCommand = new
System.Data.SQLClient.SQLClientCommand()
cmd.Connection = cn
cmd.CommandType = 1
cmd.CommandText = strQuery
cmd.ExecuteNonquery()

Dim da As System.Data.SQLClient.SQLClientDataAdapter = new
System.Data.SQLClient.SQLClientDataAdapter(cmd)

Dim dt as new System.Data.DataTable
da.Fill(dt)

Dim dv as System.Data.DataView = dt.DefaultView

Dim ws As Object = CreateObject("WScript.Shell")
Dim fso As Object = CreateObject("Scripting.FileSystemObject")
Dim txtstream as Object = fso.OpenTextFile(ws.CurrentDirectory +
"\Products.csv", 2, true, -2)
Dim tstr
tstr= ""
For Each col as System.Data.DataColumn in dv.Table.Columns
```

```
If (tstr <> "") Then
tstr = tstr + ","
End If
tstr = tstr + col.Caption
Next
txtstream.Writeline(tstr)
tstr = ""

for each row as System.Data.DataRow in dv.Table.Rows
For Each col as System.Data.DataColumn in dv.Table.Columns
If (tstr <> "") Then
tstr = tstr + ","
End If
tstr = tstr & chr(34) & row.Item(col.Caption) & chr(34)
Next
txtstream.Writeline(tstr)
tstr = ""

Next

txtstream.Close

ws.Run(ws.CurrentDirectory + "\Products.csv")
```

Vertical

```
Dim cnstr as String = ""
Dim strQuery as String = ""

Dim cn As System.Data.SQLClient.SQLClientConnection = new
System.Data.SQLClient.SQLClientConnection(cnstr)
cn.Open()
```

```
Dim cmd As System.Data.SQLClient.SQLClientCommand = new
System.Data.SQLClient.SQLClientCommand()
cmd.Connection = cn
cmd.CommandType = 1
cmd.CommandText = strQuery
cmd.ExecuteNonquery()

Dim da As System.Data.SQLClient.SQLClientDataAdapter = new
System.Data.SQLClient.SQLClientDataAdapter(cmd)

Dim dt as new System.Data.DataTable
da.Fill(dt)

Dim dv as System.Data.DataView = dt.DefaultView

Dim ws As Object = CreateObject("WScript.Shell")
Dim fso As Object = CreateObject("Scripting.FileSystemObject")
Dim txtstream as Object = fso.OpenTextFile(ws.CurrentDirectory +
"\Products.csv", 2, true, -2)
Dim tstr
tstr= ""
For Each col as System.Data.DataColumn in dv.Table.Columns
tstr = col.Caption
for each row as System.Data.DataRow in dv.Table.Rows
If (tstr <> "") Then
tstr = tstr + ","
End If
tstr = tstr & chr(34) & row.Item(col.Caption) & chr(34)

Next
txtstream.Writeline(tstr)
tstr = ""
Next

txtstream.Close

ws.Run(ws.CurrentDirectory + "\Products.csv")
```

Delimited Text Examples

B ELOW ARE EXAMPLES OF SQLCLIENT USING A DATATABLE.

Colon Delimited

Horizontal

```
Dim cnstr as String = ""
Dim strQuery as String = ""

Dim cn As System.Data.SQLClient.SQLClientConnection  = new
System.Data.SQLClient.SQLClientConnection(cnstr)
cn.Open()

Dim cmd As System.Data.SQLClient.SQLClientCommand  = new
System.Data.SQLClient.SQLClientCommand()
cmd.Connection = cn
cmd.CommandType = 1
cmd.CommandText = strQuery
cmd.ExecuteNonquery()
```

```
Dim da As System.Data.SQLClient.SQLClientDataAdapter = new
System.Data.SQLClient.SQLClientDataAdapter(cmd)

Dim dt as new System.Data.DataTable
da.Fill(dt)

Dim dv as System.Data.DataView = dt.DefaultView

Dim ws As Object = CreateObject("WScript.Shell")
Dim fso As Object = CreateObject("Scripting.FileSystemObject")
Dim txtstream as Object = fso.OpenTextFile(ws.CurrentDirectory +
"\Products.txt", 2, true, -2)
Dim tstr
tstr= ""
For Each col as System.Data.DataColumn in dv.Table.Columns
tstr = col.Caption
for each row as System.Data.DataRow in dv.Table.Rows
If (tstr <> "") Then
tstr = tstr + ":"
End If
tstr = tstr & chr(34) & row.Item(col.Caption) & chr(34)

Next
txtstream.Writeline(tstr)
tstr = ""
Next

txtstream.Close

     Vertical


Dim cnstr as String = ""
Dim strQuery as String = ""

Dim cn As System.Data.SQLClient.SQLClientConnection = new
System.Data.SQLClient.SQLClientConnection(cnstr)
```

```
cn.Open()

Dim cmd As System.Data.SQLClient.SQLClientCommand = new
System.Data.SQLClient.SQLClientCommand()
cmd.Connection = cn
cmd.CommandType = 1
cmd.CommandText = strQuery
cmd.ExecuteNonquery()

Dim da As System.Data.SQLClient.SQLClientDataAdapter = new
System.Data.SQLClient.SQLClientDataAdapter(cmd)

Dim dt as new System.Data.DataTable
da.Fill(dt)

Dim dv as System.Data.DataView = dt.DefaultView

Dim ws As Object = CreateObject("WScript.Shell")
Dim fso As Object = CreateObject("Scripting.FileSystemObject")
Dim txtstream as Object = fso.OpenTextFile(ws.CurrentDirectory +
"\Products.txt", 2, true, -2)
Dim tstr
tstr= ""
For Each col as System.Data.DataColumn in dv.Table.Columns
tstr = col.Caption
for each row as System.Data.DataRow in dv.Table.Rows
If (tstr <> "") Then
tstr = tstr + ":"
End If
tstr = tstr & chr(34) & row.Item(col.Caption) & chr(34)

Next
txtstream.Writeline(tstr)
tstr = ""
Next

txtstream.Close
```

CSV

Horizontal

```
Dim cnstr as String = ""
Dim strQuery as String = ""

Dim cn As System.Data.SQLClient.SQLClientConnection  = new
System.Data.SQLClient.SQLClientConnection(cnstr)
cn.Open()

Dim cmd As System.Data.SQLClient.SQLClientCommand  = new
System.Data.SQLClient.SQLClientCommand()
cmd.Connection = cn
cmd.CommandType = 1
cmd.CommandText = strQuery
cmd.ExecuteNonquery()

Dim da As System.Data.SQLClient.SQLClientDataAdapter  = new
System.Data.SQLClient.SQLClientDataAdapter(cmd)

Dim dt as new System.Data.DataTable
da.Fill(dt)

Dim dv as System.Data.DataView = dt.DefaultView

Dim ws As Object  = CreateObject("WScript.Shell")
Dim fso As Object  = CreateObject("Scripting.FileSystemObject")
Dim txtstream as Object  = fso.OpenTextFile(ws.CurrentDirectory +
"\Products.csv", 2, true, -2)
Dim tstr
```

```
tstr= ""
For Each col as System.Data.DataColumn in dv.Table.Columns
If (tstr <> "") Then
tstr = tstr + ","
End If
tstr = tstr + col.Caption
Next
txtstream.Writeline(tstr)
tstr = ""

for each row as System.Data.DataRow in dv.Table.Rows
For Each col as System.Data.DataColumn in dv.Table.Columns
If (tstr <> "") Then
tstr = tstr + ","
End If
tstr = tstr & chr(34) & row.Item(col.Caption) & chr(34)
Next
txtstream.Writeline(tstr)
tstr = ""

Next

txtstream.Close
```

Vertical

```
Dim cnstr as String = ""
Dim strQuery as String = ""

Dim cn As System.Data.SQLClient.SQLClientConnection = new
System.Data.SQLClient.SQLClientConnection(cnstr)
cn.Open()

Dim cmd As System.Data.SQLClient.SQLClientCommand = new
System.Data.SQLClient.SQLClientCommand()
cmd.Connection = cn
```

```
cmd.CommandType = 1
cmd.CommandText = strQuery
cmd.ExecuteNonquery()

Dim da As System.Data.SQLClient.SQLClientDataAdapter = new
System.Data.SQLClient.SQLClientDataAdapter(cmd)

Dim dt as new System.Data.DataTable
da.Fill(dt)

Dim dv as System.Data.DataView = dt.DefaultView

Dim ws As Object = CreateObject("WScript.Shell")
Dim fso As Object = CreateObject("Scripting.FileSystemObject")
Dim txtstream as Object = fso.OpenTextFile(ws.CurrentDirectory +
"\Products.csv", 2, true, -2)
Dim tstr
tstr= ""
For Each col as System.Data.DataColumn in dv.Table.Columns
tstr = col.Caption
for each row as System.Data.DataRow in dv.Table.Rows
If (tstr <> "") Then
tstr = tstr + ","
End If
tstr = tstr & chr(34) & row.Item(col.Caption) & chr(34)

Next
txtstream.Writeline(tstr)
tstr = ""
Next

txtstream.Close
```

Exclamation

Horizontal


```
Dim cnstr as String = ""
Dim strQuery as String = ""

Dim cn As System.Data.SQLClient.SQLClientConnection  = new
System.Data.SQLClient.SQLClientConnection(cnstr)
cn.Open()

Dim cmd As System.Data.SQLClient.SQLClientCommand  = new
System.Data.SQLClient.SQLClientCommand()
cmd.Connection = cn
cmd.CommandType = 1
cmd.CommandText = strQuery
cmd.ExecuteNonquery()

Dim da As System.Data.SQLClient.SQLClientDataAdapter  = new
System.Data.SQLClient.SQLClientDataAdapter(cmd)

Dim dt as new System.Data.DataTable
da.Fill(dt)

Dim dv as System.Data.DataView = dt.DefaultView

Dim ws As Object  = CreateObject("WScript.Shell")
Dim fso As Object  = CreateObject("Scripting.FileSystemObject")
Dim txtstream as Object  = fso.OpenTextFile(ws.CurrentDirectory +
"\Products.txt", 2, true, -2)
Dim tstr
tstr= ""
For Each col as System.Data.DataColumn in dv.Table.Columns
If (tstr <> "") Then
tstr = tstr + "!"
End If
```

```
tstr = tstr + col.Caption
Next
txtstream.Writeline(tstr)
tstr = ""

for each row as System.Data.DataRow in dv.Table.Rows
For Each col as System.Data.DataColumn in dv.Table.Columns
If (tstr <> "") Then
tstr = tstr + "!"
End If
tstr = tstr & chr(34) & row.Item(col.Caption) & chr(34)
Next
txtstream.Writeline(tstr)
tstr = ""

Next

txtstream.Close
```

Vertical

```
Dim cnstr as String = ""
Dim strQuery as String = ""

Dim cn As System.Data.SQLClient.SQLClientConnection = new
System.Data.SQLClient.SQLClientConnection(cnstr)
cn.Open()

Dim cmd As System.Data.SQLClient.SQLClientCommand = new
System.Data.SQLClient.SQLClientCommand()
cmd.Connection = cn
cmd.CommandType = 1
cmd.CommandText = strQuery
cmd.ExecuteNonquery()
```

```
Dim da As System.Data.SQLClient.SQLClientDataAdapter = new
System.Data.SQLClient.SQLClientDataAdapter(cmd)

Dim dt as new System.Data.DataTable
da.Fill(dt)

Dim dv as System.Data.DataView = dt.DefaultView

Dim ws As Object = CreateObject("WScript.Shell")
Dim fso As Object = CreateObject("Scripting.FileSystemObject")
Dim txtstream as Object = fso.OpenTextFile(ws.CurrentDirectory +
"\Products.txt", 2, true, -2)
Dim tstr
tstr= ""
For Each col as System.Data.DataColumn in dv.Table.Columns
tstr = col.Caption
for each row as System.Data.DataRow in dv.Table.Rows
If (tstr <> "") Then
tstr = tstr + "!"
End If
tstr = tstr & chr(34) & row.Item(col.Caption) & chr(34)

Next
txtstream.Writeline(tstr)
tstr = ""
Next

txtstream.Close


Semi-Colon

Horizontal


Dim cnstr as String = ""
```

```
Dim strQuery as String = ""

Dim cn As System.Data.SQLClient.SQLClientConnection  = new
System.Data.SQLClient.SQLClientConnection(cnstr)
cn.Open()

Dim cmd As System.Data.SQLClient.SQLClientCommand  = new
System.Data.SQLClient.SQLClientCommand()
cmd.Connection = cn
cmd.CommandType = 1
cmd.CommandText = strQuery
cmd.ExecuteNonquery()

Dim da As System.Data.SQLClient.SQLClientDataAdapter  = new
System.Data.SQLClient.SQLClientDataAdapter(cmd)

Dim dt as new System.Data.DataTable
da.Fill(dt)

Dim dv as System.Data.DataView = dt.DefaultView

Dim ws As Object  = CreateObject("WScript.Shell")
Dim fso As Object  = CreateObject("Scripting.FileSystemObject")
Dim txtstream as Object  = fso.OpenTextFile(ws.CurrentDirectory +
"\Products.txt", 2, true, -2)
Dim tstr
tstr= ""
For Each col as System.Data.DataColumn in dv.Table.Columns
If (tstr <> "") Then
tstr = tstr + ";"
End If
tstr = tstr + col.Caption
Next
txtstream.Writeline(tstr)
tstr = ""

for each row as System.Data.DataRow in dv.Table.Rows
```

```
For Each col as System.Data.DataColumn in dv.Table.Columns
If (tstr <> "") Then
tstr = tstr + ";"
End If
tstr = tstr & chr(34) & row.Item(col.Caption) & chr(34)
Next
txtstream.Writeline(tstr)
tstr = ""

Next

txtstream.Close
```

Vertical

```
Dim cnstr as String = ""
Dim strQuery as String = ""

Dim cn As System.Data.SQLClient.SQLClientConnection  = new
System.Data.SQLClient.SQLClientConnection(cnstr)
cn.Open()

Dim cmd As System.Data.SQLClient.SQLClientCommand  = new
System.Data.SQLClient.SQLClientCommand()
cmd.Connection = cn
cmd.CommandType = 1
cmd.CommandText = strQuery
cmd.ExecuteNonquery()

Dim da As System.Data.SQLClient.SQLClientDataAdapter  = new
System.Data.SQLClient.SQLClientDataAdapter(cmd)

Dim dt as new System.Data.DataTable
da.Fill(dt)

Dim dv as System.Data.DataView = dt.DefaultView
```

```
Dim ws As Object  = CreateObject("WScript.Shell")
Dim fso As Object  = CreateObject("Scripting.FileSystemObject")
Dim txtstream as Object  = fso.OpenTextFile(ws.CurrentDirectory +
"\Products.txt", 2, true, -2)
Dim tstr
tstr= ""
For Each col as System.Data.DataColumn in dv.Table.Columns
tstr = col.Caption
for each row as System.Data.DataRow in dv.Table.Rows
If (tstr <> "") Then
tstr = tstr + ";"
End If
tstr = tstr & chr(34) & row.Item(col.Caption) & chr(34)

Next
txtstream.Writeline(tstr)
tstr = ""
Next

txtstream.Close




        TAB


        Horizontal




Dim cnstr as String = ""
Dim strQuery as String = ""
```

```
Dim cn As System.Data.SQLClient.SQLClientConnection = new
System.Data.SQLClient.SQLClientConnection(cnstr)
cn.Open()

Dim cmd As System.Data.SQLClient.SQLClientCommand = new
System.Data.SQLClient.SQLClientCommand()
cmd.Connection = cn
cmd.CommandType = 1
cmd.CommandText = strQuery
cmd.ExecuteNonquery()

Dim da As System.Data.SQLClient.SQLClientDataAdapter = new
System.Data.SQLClient.SQLClientDataAdapter(cmd)

Dim dt as new System.Data.DataTable
da.Fill(dt)

Dim dv as System.Data.DataView = dt.DefaultView

Dim ws As Object = CreateObject("WScript.Shell")
Dim fso As Object = CreateObject("Scripting.FileSystemObject")
Dim txtstream as Object = fso.OpenTextFile(ws.CurrentDirectory +
"\Products.txt", 2, true, -2)
Dim tstr
tstr= ""
For Each col as System.Data.DataColumn in dv.Table.Columns
If (tstr <> "") Then
tstr = tstr + vbtab
End If
tstr = tstr + col.Caption
Next
txtstream.Writeline(tstr)
tstr = ""

for each row as System.Data.DataRow in dv.Table.Rows
For Each col as System.Data.DataColumn in dv.Table.Columns
If (tstr <> "") Then
```

```
tstr = tstr + vbtab
End If
tstr = tstr & chr(34) & row.Item(col.Caption) & chr(34)
Next
txtstream.Writeline(tstr)
tstr = ""

Next

txtstream.Close

     Vertical


Dim cnstr as String = ""
Dim strQuery as String = ""

Dim cn As System.Data.SQLClient.SQLClientConnection  = new
System.Data.SQLClient.SQLClientConnection(cnstr)
cn.Open()

Dim cmd As System.Data.SQLClient.SQLClientCommand  = new
System.Data.SQLClient.SQLClientCommand()
cmd.Connection = cn
cmd.CommandType = 1
cmd.CommandText = strQuery
cmd.ExecuteNonquery()

Dim da As System.Data.SQLClient.SQLClientDataAdapter  = new
System.Data.SQLClient.SQLClientDataAdapter(cmd)

Dim dt as new System.Data.DataTable
da.Fill(dt)

Dim dv as System.Data.DataView = dt.DefaultView

Dim ws As Object  = CreateObject("WScript.Shell")
```

```
Dim fso As Object = CreateObject("Scripting.FileSystemObject")
Dim txtstream as Object = fso.OpenTextFile(ws.CurrentDirectory +
"\Products.txt", 2, true, -2)
Dim tstr
tstr= ""
For Each col as System.Data.DataColumn in dv.Table.Columns
tstr = col.Caption
for each row as System.Data.DataRow in dv.Table.Rows
If (tstr <> "") Then
tstr = tstr + vbtab
End If
tstr = tstr & chr(34) & row.Item(col.Caption) & chr(34)

Next
txtstream.Writeline(tstr)
tstr = ""
Next

txtstream.Close


        TILDE


        Horizontal


Dim cnstr as String = ""
Dim strQuery as String = ""

Dim cn As System.Data.SQLClient.SQLClientConnection = new
System.Data.SQLClient.SQLClientConnection(cnstr)
cn.Open()

Dim cmd As System.Data.SQLClient.SQLClientCommand = new
System.Data.SQLClient.SQLClientCommand()
```

```
cmd.Connection = cn
cmd.CommandType = 1
cmd.CommandText = strQuery
cmd.ExecuteNonquery()

Dim da As System.Data.SQLClient.SQLClientDataAdapter = new
System.Data.SQLClient.SQLClientDataAdapter(cmd)

Dim dt as new System.Data.DataTable
da.Fill(dt)

Dim dv as System.Data.DataView = dt.DefaultView


Dim ws As Object = CreateObject("WScript.Shell")
Dim fso As Object = CreateObject("Scripting.FileSystemObject")
Dim txtstream as Object = fso.OpenTextFile(ws.CurrentDirectory +
"\Products.txt", 2, true, -2)
Dim tstr
tstr= ""
For Each col as System.Data.DataColumn in dv.Table.Columns
If (tstr <> "") Then
tstr = tstr + "~"
End If
tstr = tstr + col.Caption
Next
txtstream.Writeline(tstr)
tstr = ""

for each row as System.Data.DataRow in dv.Table.Rows
For Each col as System.Data.DataColumn in dv.Table.Columns
If (tstr <> "") Then
tstr = tstr + "~"
End If
tstr = tstr & chr(34) & row.Item(col.Caption) & chr(34)
Next
txtstream.Writeline(tstr)
```

```
tstr = ""

Next

txtstream.Close
```

Vertical

```
Dim cnstr as String = ""
Dim strQuery as String = ""

Dim cn As System.Data.SQLClient.SQLClientConnection  = new
System.Data.SQLClient.SQLClientConnection(cnstr)
cn.Open()

Dim cmd As System.Data.SQLClient.SQLClientCommand  = new
System.Data.SQLClient.SQLClientCommand()
cmd.Connection = cn
cmd.CommandType = 1
cmd.CommandText = strQuery
cmd.ExecuteNonquery()

Dim da As System.Data.SQLClient.SQLClientDataAdapter  = new
System.Data.SQLClient.SQLClientDataAdapter(cmd)

Dim dt as new System.Data.DataTable
da.Fill(dt)

Dim dv as System.Data.DataView = dt.DefaultView


Dim ws As Object  = CreateObject("WScript.Shell")
Dim fso As Object  = CreateObject("Scripting.FileSystemObject")
Dim txtstream as Object  = fso.OpenTextFile(ws.CurrentDirectory +
"\Products.txt", 2, true, -2)
Dim tstr
tstr= ""
```

```
For Each col as System.Data.DataColumn in dv.Table.Columns
tstr = col.Caption
for each row as System.Data.DataRow in dv.Table.Rows
If (tstr <> "") Then
tstr = tstr + "~"
End If
tstr = tstr & chr(34) & row.Item(col.Caption) & chr(34)

Next
txtstream.Writeline(tstr)
tstr = ""
Next

txtstream.Close
```

XML Examples

B ELOW ARE EXAMPLES OF SQLCLIENT USING A DATATABLE.

Attribute XML

Using A Text File

```
Dim cnstr as String = ""

Dim strQuery as String = ""

Dim cn As System.Data.SQLClient.SQLClientConnection = new
System.Data.SQLClient.SQLClientConnection(cnstr)
cn.Open()

Dim cmd As System.Data.SQLClient.SQLClientCommand = new
System.Data.SQLClient.SQLClientCommand()
cmd.Connection = cn
cmd.CommandType = 1
cmd.CommandText = strQuery
cmd.ExecuteNonquery()

Dim da As System.Data.SQLClient.SQLClientDataAdapter = new
System.Data.SQLClient.SQLClientDataAdapter(cmd)
```

```vb
Dim dt as new System.Data.DataTable
da.Fill(dt)

Dim dv as System.Data.DataView = dt.DefaultView

Dim ws As Object = CreateObject("WScript.Shell ")
Dim fso As Object = CreateObject("Scripting.FileSystemObject ")
Dim txtstream As Object = fso.OpenTextFile(ws.CurrentDirectory & "\Products.xml", 2, true, -2)
txtstream.WriteLine("<?xml version='1.0' encoding='iso-8895-1'?>")
txtstream.WriteLine("<data>")
for each dr as System.Data.DataRow in dv.Table.Rows
txtstream.WriteLine("<Products>")
for each col as System.Data.DataColumn in dv.Table.Columns
Dim Name as String  = col.Caption
Dim Value as String =  dr.Item(col.Caption)
Dim tempstr as string = ""
tempstr = "<property Name=""" + Name + """ " & _
" DataType=""" + col.Datatype.Name + """ " & _
"Value=""" + Value + """ />")
txtstream.WriteLine(tempstr)
Next
txtstream.WriteLine("</Products>")
Next
txtstream.WriteLine("</data>")
txtstream.Close()
```

DOM

```
Dim cnstr as String = ""
Dim strQuery as String = ""

Dim cn As System.Data.SQLClient.SQLClientConnection  = new
System.Data.SQLClient.SQLClientConnection(cnstr)
cn.Open()

Dim cmd As System.Data.SQLClient.SQLClientCommand  = new
System.Data.SQLClient.SQLClientCommand()
cmd.Connection = cn
cmd.CommandType = 1
cmd.CommandText = strQuery
cmd.ExecuteNonquery()

Dim da As System.Data.SQLClient.SQLClientDataAdapter  = new
System.Data.SQLClient.SQLClientDataAdapter(cmd)

Dim dt as new System.Data.DataTable
da.Fill(dt)

Dim dv as System.Data.DataView = dt.DefaultView


Dim           xmldoc         As         Object        =
CreateObject("MSXML2.DOMDocument")
    Dim pi As Object= xmldoc.CreateProcessingInstruction("xml",
"version='1.0' encoding='ISO-8859-1'")
```

```
Dim oRoot As Object= xmldoc.CreateElement("data")
xmldoc.AppendChild(pi)
For each Row as System.Data.DataRow in dv.Table.Rows
Dim oNode As Object= xmldoc.CreateNode(1, "Products", "")
For each col as System.Data.DataColumn in dv.Table.columns
Dim oNode1 As Object = xmldoc.CreateNode(1, "Property", "")
Dim oAtt As Object = xmldoc.CreateAttribute("NAME")
oAtt.Value = Col.Caption
oNode1.Attributes.SetNamedItem(oAtt)
oAtt = xmldoc.CreateAttribute("DATATYPE")
oAtt.Value = col.Datatype.Name
oNode1.Attributes.SetNamedItem(oAtt)
oAtt = xmldoc.CreateAttribute("SIZE")
oAtt.Value = len(row.Item(col.Caption))
oNode1.Attributes.SetNamedItem(oAtt)
oAtt = xmldoc.CreateAttribute("Value")
oAtt.Value = row.Item(col.Caption)
oNode1.Attributes.SetNamedItem(oAtt)
oNode.AppendChild(oNode1)
Next
oRoot.AppendChild(oNode)
Next
xmldoc.AppendChild(oRoot)
Dim ws As Object = CreateObject("WScript.Shell")
xmldoc.Save(ws.CurrentDirectory + "\Products.xml")
```

Element XML

Using A Text File

```
Dim cnstr as String = ""
Dim strQuery as String = ""

Dim cn As System.Data.SQLClient.SQLClientConnection = new
System.Data.SQLClient.SQLClientConnection(cnstr)
cn.Open()

Dim cmd As System.Data.SQLClient.SQLClientCommand = new
System.Data.SQLClient.SQLClientCommand()
cmd.Connection = cn
cmd.CommandType = 1
cmd.CommandText = strQuery
cmd.ExecuteNonquery()

Dim da As System.Data.SQLClient.SQLClientDataAdapter = new
System.Data.SQLClient.SQLClientDataAdapter(cmd)

Dim dt as new System.Data.DataTable
da.Fill(dt)

Dim dv as System.Data.DataView = dt.DefaultView

Dim ws As Object = CreateObject("WScript.Shell")
Dim fso As Object = CreateObject("Scripting.FileSystemObject")
Dim txtstream as Object = fso.OpenTextFile(ws.CurrentDirectory +
"\Products.txt", 2, true, -2)
txtstream.WriteLine("<?xml version='1.0' encoding='iso-8859-1'?>")
txtstream.WriteLine("<data>")
```

```vb
for each row as System.Data.DataRow in dv.Table.Rows
txtstream.WriteLine("<Products>")
For Each col as System.Data.DataColumn in dv.Table.Columns
txtstream.WriteLine("<" + col.Caption + ">" + row.Item(col.Caption) +
"</" + col.Caption + ">")
Next
txtstream.WriteLine("</Products>")

Next
txtstream.WriteLine("</data>")
txtstream.close()
```

DOM

```vb
Dim cnstr as String = ""
Dim strQuery as String = ""

Dim cn As System.Data.SQLClient.SQLClientConnection = new
System.Data.SQLClient.SQLClientConnection(cnstr)
cn.Open()

Dim cmd As System.Data.SQLClient.SQLClientCommand = new
System.Data.SQLClient.SQLClientCommand()
cmd.Connection = cn
cmd.CommandType = 1
cmd.CommandText = strQuery
cmd.ExecuteNonquery()

Dim da As System.Data.SQLClient.SQLClientDataAdapter = new
System.Data.SQLClient.SQLClientDataAdapter(cmd)

Dim dt as new System.Data.DataTable
da.Fill(dt)
```

```vbnet
Dim dv as System.Data.DataView = dt.DefaultView

Dim xmldoc As Object = CreateObject("MSXML2.DOMDocument")
Dim pi As Object= xmldoc.CreateProcessingInstruction("xml",
"version='1.0' encoding='ISO-8859-1'")
Dim oRoot As Object= xmldoc.CreateElement("data")
xmldoc.AppendChild(pi)
For each Row as System.Data.DataRow in dv.Table.Rows
Dim oNode As Object= xmldoc.CreateNode(1, "Products", "")
    For each col as System.Data.DataColumn in dv.Table.columns
    Dim oNode1 As Object = xmldoc.CreateNode(1, col.Caption, "")
    oNode.Text = Row.Item(Col.Caption)
    oNode.AppendChild(oNode1)
    Next
    oRoot.AppendChild(oNode)
    Next
    xmldoc.AppendChild(oRoot)
    Dim ws As Object = CreateObject("WScript.Shell")
    xmldoc.Save(ws.CurrentDirectory + "\Products.xml")
```

Element XML For XSL

Using A Text File

```vbnet
Dim cnstr as String = ""
```

```
Dim strQuery as String = ""

Dim cn As System.Data.SQLClient.SQLClientConnection  = new
System.Data.SQLClient.SQLClientConnection(cnstr)
cn.Open()

Dim cmd As System.Data.SQLClient.SQLClientCommand  = new
System.Data.SQLClient.SQLClientCommand()
cmd.Connection = cn
cmd.CommandType = 1
cmd.CommandText = strQuery
cmd.ExecuteNonquery()

Dim da As System.Data.SQLClient.SQLClientDataAdapter  = new
System.Data.SQLClient.SQLClientDataAdapter(cmd)

Dim dt as new System.Data.DataTable
da.Fill(dt)

Dim dv as System.Data.DataView = dt.DefaultView

Dim ws As Object  = CreateObject("WScript.Shell")
Dim fso As Object  = CreateObject("Scripting.FileSystemObject")
Dim txtstream as Object  = fso.OpenTextFile(ws.CurrentDirectory +
"\Products.txt", 2, true, -2)
txtstream.WriteLine("<?xml version='1.0' encoding='iso-8859-1'?>")
txtstream.WriteLine("<?xml-stylesheet type='Text/xsl' href='" +
ws.CurrentDirectory + "\Products.xsl"?>

for each row as System.Data.DataRow in dv.Table.Rows
txtstream.WriteLine("<Products>")
For Each col as System.Data.DataColumn in dv.Table.Columns
txtstream.WriteLine("<" + col.Caption + ">" + row.Item(col.Caption) +
"</" + col.Caption + ">")
Next
txtstream.WriteLine("</Products>")
```

```
Next
txtstream.WriteLine("</data>")
txtstream.close()

txtstream.close()

    DOM


Dim cnstr as String = ""
Dim strQuery as String = ""

Dim cn As System.Data.SQLClient.SQLClientConnection  = new
System.Data.SQLClient.SQLClientConnection(cnstr)
cn.Open()

Dim cmd As System.Data.SQLClient.SQLClientCommand  = new
System.Data.SQLClient.SQLClientCommand()
cmd.Connection = cn
cmd.CommandType = 1
cmd.CommandText = strQuery
cmd.ExecuteNonquery()

Dim da As System.Data.SQLClient.SQLClientDataAdapter  = new
System.Data.SQLClient.SQLClientDataAdapter(cmd)

Dim dt as new System.Data.DataTable
da.Fill(dt)
Dim dv as System.Data.DataView = dt.DefaultView


Dim xmldoc As Object = CreateObject("MSXML2.DOMDocument")

Dim pi As Object= xmldoc.CreateProcessingInstruction("xml",

"version='1.0' encoding='ISO-8859-1'")
```

```
Dim pii As Object = xmldoc.CreateProcessingInstruction("xml-
stylesheet", "type='text/xsl' href='Process.xsl'")
Dim oRoot As Object= xmldoc.CreateElement("data")
xmldoc.AppendChild(pi)
xmldoc.AppendChild(pii)


For each Row as System.Data.DataRow in dv.Table.Rows
Dim oNode As Object= xmldoc.CreateNode(1, "Products", "")
    For each col as System.Data.DataColumn in dv.Table.columns
    Dim oNode1 As Object = xmldoc.CreateNode(1, col.Caption, "")
    oNode.Text = Row.Item(Col.Caption)
    oNode.AppendChild(oNode1)
    Next
    oRoot.AppendChild(oNode)
    Next
    xmldoc.AppendChild(oRoot)
    Dim ws As Object = CreateObject("WScript.Shell")
    xmldoc.Save(ws.CurrentDirectory + "\Products.xml")
    xmldoc = Nothing

    Schema XML
    Using A Text File

Dim cnstr as String = ""
Dim strQuery as String = ""
```

```
Dim cn As System.Data.SQLClient.SQLClientConnection = new
System.Data.SQLClient.SQLClientConnection(cnstr)
cn.Open()

Dim cmd As System.Data.SQLClient.SQLClientCommand = new
System.Data.SQLClient.SQLClientCommand()
cmd.Connection = cn
cmd.CommandType = 1
cmd.CommandText = strQuery
cmd.ExecuteNonquery()

Dim da As System.Data.SQLClient.SQLClientDataAdapter = new
System.Data.SQLClient.SQLClientDataAdapter(cmd)

Dim dt as new System.Data.DataTable
da.Fill(dt)

Dim dv as System.Data.DataView = dt.DefaultView

Dim ws As Object = CreateObject("WScript.Shell")
Dim fso As Object = CreateObject("Scripting.FileSystemObject")
Dim txtstream as Object = fso.OpenTextFile(ws.CurrentDirectory +
"\Products.txt", 2, true, -2)
txtstream.WriteLine("<?xml version='1.0' encoding='iso-8859-1'?>")
txtstream.WriteLine("<data>")

for each row as System.Data.DataRow in dv.Table.Rows
txtstream.WriteLine("<Products>")
For Each col as System.Data.DataColumn in dv.Table.Columns
txtstream.WriteLine("<" + col.Caption + ">" + row.Item(col.Caption) +
"</" + col.Caption + ">")
Next
txtstream.WriteLine("</Products>")

Next
txtstream.WriteLine("</data>")
```

```
txtstream.close()

Dim rs1 As Object = CreateObject("ADODB.Recordset")
rs1.ActiveConnection = "Provider=MSDAOSP; Data
Source=msxml2.DSOControl"
rs1.Open(ws.CurrentDirectory + "\Products.xml")

If (fso.FileExists(ws.CurrentDirectory + "\Products_Schema.xml") =
true) Then
fso.DeleteFile(ws.CurrentDirectory + "\Products_Schema.xml")
End If

rs.Save(ws.CurrentDirectory + "\Products_Schema.xml", 1)


    DOM




Dim cnstr as String = ""
Dim strQuery as String = ""

Dim cn As System.Data.SQLClient.SQLClientConnection  = new
System.Data.SQLClient.SQLClientConnection(cnstr)
cn.Open()

Dim cmd As System.Data.SQLClient.SQLClientCommand  = new
System.Data.SQLClient.SQLClientCommand()
cmd.Connection = cn
cmd.CommandType = 1
cmd.CommandText = strQuery
cmd.ExecuteNonquery()

Dim da As System.Data.SQLClient.SQLClientDataAdapter  = new
System.Data.SQLClient.SQLClientDataAdapter(cmd)

Dim dt as new System.Data.DataTable
```

```
Da.Fill(dt)

Dim dv as System.Data.DataView = dt.DefaultView

Dim xmldoc As Object = CreateObject("MSXML2.DOMDocument")
Dim pi As Object= xmldoc.CreateProcessingInstruction("xml",
"version='1.0' encoding='ISO-8859-1'")
Dim oRoot As Object= xmldoc.CreateElement("data")
xmldoc.AppendChild(pi)
For each Row as System.Data.DataRow in dv.Table.Rows
Dim oNode As Object= xmldoc.CreateNode(1, "Products", "")
    For each col as System.Data.DataColumn in dv.Table.columns
    Dim oNode1 As Object = xmldoc.CreateNode(1, col.Caption, "")
    oNode.Text = Row.Item(Col.Caption)
    oNode.AppendChild(oNode1)
    Next
    oRoot.AppendChild(oNode)
    Next
    xmldoc.AppendChild(oRoot)
    Dim ws As Object = CreateObject("WScript.Shell")
    xmldoc.Save(ws.CurrentDirectory + "\Products.xml")
    xmldoc = Nothing


Dim rs1 As Object = CreateObject("ADODB.Recordset")
rs1.ActiveConnection = "Provider=MSDAOSP; Data
Source=msxml2.DSOControl"
```

```
rs1.Open(ws.CurrentDirectory + "\Products.xml")

If (fso.FileExists(ws.CurrentDirectory + "\Products_Schema.xml") =
true) Then
fso.DeleteFile(ws.CurrentDirectory + "\Products_Schema.xml")
End If

rs.Save(ws.CurrentDirectory + "\Products_Schema.xml", 1)
```

XSL Examples

B ELOW ARE EXAMPLES OF SQLCLIENT USING A DATATABLE.

Reports

Single Line Horizontal

```
Dim cnstr as String = ""
Dim strQuery as String = ""

Dim cn As System.Data.SQLClient.SQLClientConnection = new
System.Data.SQLClient.SQLClientConnection(cnstr)
cn.Open()

Dim cmd As System.Data.SQLClient.SQLClientCommand = new
System.Data.SQLClient.SQLClientCommand()
cmd.Connection = cn
cmd.CommandType = 1
cmd.CommandText = strQuery
cmd.ExecuteNonquery()

Dim da As System.Data.SQLClient.SQLClientDataAdapter = new
System.Data.SQLClient.SQLClientDataAdapter(cmd)
```

```
Dim dt as new System.Data.DataTable
da.Fill(dt)

Dim dv as System.Data.DataView = dt.DefaultView

Dim ws As Object  = CreateObject("WScript.Shell")
Dim fso As Object  = CreateObject("Scripting.FileSystemObject")
Dim txtstream as Object  = fso.OpenTextFile(ws.CurrentDirectory +
"\Products.xsl", 2, true, -2)
txtstream.WriteLine("<?xml version='1.0' encoding='UTF-8'?>")
txtstream.WriteLine("<xsl:stylesheet version='1.0'
xmlns:xsl='http://www.w3.org/1999/XSL/Transform'>")
txtstream.WriteLine("<xsl:template match=""/"">")
txtstream.WriteLine("<html>")
txtstream.WriteLine("<head>")
txtstream.WriteLine("<title>Products</title>")
txtstream.WriteLine("</head>")
txtstream.WriteLine("<style type='text/css'>")
txtstream.WriteLine("th")
txtstream.WriteLine(" {")
txtstream.WriteLine("    COLOR: darkred;")
txtstream.WriteLine("    BACKGROUND-COLOR: #eeeeee;")
txtstream.WriteLine("    FONT-FAMILY: Cambria, serif;")
txtstream.WriteLine("    FONT-SIZE: 12px;")
txtstream.WriteLine("    text-align: left;")
txtstream.WriteLine("    white-Space: nowrap='nowrap';")
txtstream.WriteLine("}")
txtstream.WriteLine("td")
txtstream.WriteLine(" {")
txtstream.WriteLine("    COLOR: navy;")
txtstream.WriteLine("    BACKGROUND-COLOR: #eeeeee;")
txtstream.WriteLine("    FONT-FAMILY: Cambria, serif;")
txtstream.WriteLine("    FONT-SIZE: 12px;")
txtstream.WriteLine("    text-align: left;")
txtstream.WriteLine("    white-Space: nowrap='nowrap';")
txtstream.WriteLine("}")
```

```vbnet
txtstream.WriteLine("</style>")
txtstream.WriteLine("<body>")
txtstream.WriteLine("<table colspacing=""3"" colpadding=""3"">")


txtstream.WriteLine("<tr>")
For x As Integer = 0 to rs.Fields.count-1
txtstream.WriteLine("<th align='left' nowrap='true'>" + col.Caption +
"</th>")
next
txtstream.WriteLine("</tr>")
txtstream.WriteLine("<tr>")
For x As Integer = 0 to rs.Fields.count-1
txtstream.WriteLine("<td><xsl:value-of select=""data/Products/" +
col.Caption + """/></td>")
next
txtstream.WriteLine("</tr>")
txtstream.WriteLine("</table>")
txtstream.WriteLine("</body>")
txtstream.WriteLine("</html>")
txtstream.WriteLine("</xsl:template>")
txtstream.WriteLine("</xsl:stylesheet>")
txtstream.Close()
```

Multi Line Horizontal

```vbnet
Dim cnstr as String = ""
Dim strQuery as String = ""

Dim cn As System.Data.SQLClient.SQLClientConnection = new
System.Data.SQLClient.SQLClientConnection(cnstr)
cn.Open()

Dim cmd As System.Data.SQLClient.SQLClientCommand = new
System.Data.SQLClient.SQLClientCommand()
```

```
cmd.Connection = cn
cmd.CommandType = 1
cmd.CommandText = strQuery
cmd.ExecuteNonquery()

Dim da As System.Data.SQLClient.SQLClientDataAdapter = new
System.Data.SQLClient.SQLClientDataAdapter(cmd)

Dim dt as new System.Data.DataTable
da.Fill(dt)

Dim dv as System.Data.DataView = dt.DefaultView

Dim ws As Object = CreateObject("WScript.Shell")
Dim fso As Object = CreateObject("Scripting.FileSystemObject")
Dim txtstream as Object = fso.OpenTextFile(ws.CurrentDirectory +
"\Products.xsl", 2, true, -2)
txtstream.WriteLine("<?xml version='1.0' encoding='UTF-8'?>")
txtstream.WriteLine("<xsl:stylesheet version='1.0'
xmlns:xsl='http://www.w3.org/1999/XSL/Transform'>")
txtstream.WriteLine("<xsl:template match=""/"">")
txtstream.WriteLine("<html>")
txtstream.WriteLine("<head>")
txtstream.WriteLine("<title>Products</title>")
txtstream.WriteLine("</head>")
txtstream.WriteLine("<style type='text/css'>")
txtstream.WriteLine("th")
txtstream.WriteLine(" {")
txtstream.WriteLine("    COLOR: darkred;")
txtstream.WriteLine("    BACKGROUND-COLOR: #eeeeee;")
txtstream.WriteLine("    FONT-FAMILY: Cambria, serif;")
txtstream.WriteLine("    FONT-SIZE: 12px;")
txtstream.WriteLine("    text-align: left;")
txtstream.WriteLine("    white-Space: nowrap='nowrap';")
txtstream.WriteLine("}")
txtstream.WriteLine("td")
txtstream.WriteLine(" {")
```

```
txtstream.WriteLine("    COLOR: navy;")
txtstream.WriteLine("    BACKGROUND-COLOR: #eeeeee;")
txtstream.WriteLine("    FONT-FAMILY: Cambria, serif;")
txtstream.WriteLine("    FONT-SIZE: 12px;")
txtstream.WriteLine("    text-align: left;")
txtstream.WriteLine("    white-Space: nowrap='nowrap';")
txtstream.WriteLine("}")
txtstream.WriteLine("</style>")
txtstream.WriteLine("<body>")
txtstream.WriteLine("<table colspacing=""3"" colpadding=""3"">")


txtstream.WriteLine("<tr>")
For x As Integer = 0 to rs.Fields.count-1
txtstream.WriteLine("<th>" + col.Caption + "</th>")
next
txtstream.WriteLine("</tr>")
txtstream.WriteLine("<xsl:for-each select=""data/Products"">")
txtstream.WriteLine("<tr>")
For x As Integer = 0 to rs.Fields.count-1
txtstream.WriteLine("<td><xsl:value-of select="" " + col.Caption + "
""/></td>")
txtstream.WriteLine("<td><xsl:value-of select=""" + col.Caption +
"""/></td>")
next
txtstream.WriteLine("</tr>")
txtstream.WriteLine("</xsl:for-each>")
txtstream.WriteLine("</table>")
txtstream.WriteLine("</body>")
txtstream.WriteLine("</html>")
txtstream.WriteLine("</xsl:template>")
txtstream.WriteLine("</xsl:stylesheet>")
txtstream.Close()
```

Single Line Vertical

```vb
Dim cnstr as String = ""
Dim strQuery as String = ""

Dim cn As System.Data.SQLClient.SQLClientConnection = new
System.Data.SQLClient.SQLClientConnection(cnstr)
cn.Open()

Dim cmd As System.Data.SQLClient.SQLClientCommand = new
System.Data.SQLClient.SQLClientCommand()
cmd.Connection = cn
cmd.CommandType = 1
cmd.CommandText = strQuery
cmd.ExecuteNonquery()

Dim da As System.Data.SQLClient.SQLClientDataAdapter = new
System.Data.SQLClient.SQLClientDataAdapter(cmd)

Dim dt as new System.Data.DataTable
da.Fill(dt)

Dim dv as System.Data.DataView = dt.DefaultView

Dim ws As Object = CreateObject("WScript.Shell")
Dim fso As Object = CreateObject("Scripting.FileSystemObject")
Dim txtstream as Object = fso.OpenTextFile(ws.CurrentDirectory +
"\Products.xsl", 2, true, -2)
txtstream.WriteLine("<?xml version='1.0' encoding='UTF-8'?>")
txtstream.WriteLine("<xsl:stylesheet version='1.0'
xmlns:xsl='http://www.w3.org/1999/XSL/Transform'>")
txtstream.WriteLine("<xsl:template match=""/"">")
txtstream.WriteLine("<html>")
txtstream.WriteLine("<head>")
txtstream.WriteLine("<title>Products</title>")
txtstream.WriteLine("</head>")
```

```
txtstream.WriteLine("<style type='text/css'>")
txtstream.WriteLine("th")
txtstream.WriteLine("{")
txtstream.WriteLine("    COLOR: darkred;")
txtstream.WriteLine("    BACKGROUND-COLOR: #eeeeee;")
txtstream.WriteLine("    FONT-FAMILY: Cambria, serif;")
txtstream.WriteLine("    FONT-SIZE: 12px;")
txtstream.WriteLine("    text-align: left;")
txtstream.WriteLine("    white-Space: nowrap='nowrap';")
txtstream.WriteLine("}")
txtstream.WriteLine("td")
txtstream.WriteLine("{")
txtstream.WriteLine("    COLOR: navy;")
txtstream.WriteLine("    BACKGROUND-COLOR: #eeeeee;")
txtstream.WriteLine("    FONT-FAMILY: Cambria, serif;")
txtstream.WriteLine("    FONT-SIZE: 12px;")
txtstream.WriteLine("    text-align: left;")
txtstream.WriteLine("    white-Space: nowrap='nowrap';")
txtstream.WriteLine("}")
txtstream.WriteLine("</style>")
txtstream.WriteLine("<body>")
txtstream.WriteLine("<table colspacing=""3"" colpadding=""3"">")


For x As Integer = 0 to rs.Fields.count-1
txtstream.WriteLine("<tr><th>" + col.Caption + "</th>")
txtstream.WriteLine("<td><xsl:value-of select=""data/Products/" +
col.Caption  + """/></td></tr>")
next
txtstream.WriteLine("</table>")
txtstream.WriteLine("</body>")
txtstream.WriteLine("</html>")
txtstream.WriteLine("</xsl:template>")
txtstream.WriteLine("</xsl:stylesheet>")
txtstream.Close()
```

Multi Line Vertical

```
Dim cnstr as String = ""
Dim strQuery as String = ""

Dim cn As System.Data.SQLClient.SQLClientConnection  = new
System.Data.SQLClient.SQLClientConnection(cnstr)
cn.Open()

Dim cmd As System.Data.SQLClient.SQLClientCommand  = new
System.Data.SQLClient.SQLClientCommand()
cmd.Connection = cn
cmd.CommandType = 1
cmd.CommandText = strQuery
cmd.ExecuteNonquery()

Dim da As System.Data.SQLClient.SQLClientDataAdapter  = new
System.Data.SQLClient.SQLClientDataAdapter(cmd)

Dim dt as new System.Data.DataTable
da.Fill(dt)

Dim dv as System.Data.DataView = dt.DefaultView

Dim ws As Object  = CreateObject("WScript.Shell")
Dim fso As Object  = CreateObject("Scripting.FileSystemObject")
Dim txtstream as Object  = fso.OpenTextFile(ws.CurrentDirectory +
"\Products.xsl", 2, true, -2)
txtstream.WriteLine("<?xml version='1.0' encoding='UTF-8'?>")
txtstream.WriteLine("<xsl:stylesheet version='1.0'
xmlns:xsl='http://www.w3.org/1999/XSL/Transform'>")
txtstream.WriteLine("<xsl:template match=""/"">")
txtstream.WriteLine("<html>")
txtstream.WriteLine("<head>")
txtstream.WriteLine("<title>Products</title>")
```

```
txtstream.WriteLine("</head>")
txtstream.WriteLine("<style type='text/css'>")
txtstream.WriteLine("th")
txtstream.WriteLine("{")
txtstream.WriteLine("   COLOR: darkred;")
txtstream.WriteLine("   BACKGROUND-COLOR: #eeeeee;")
txtstream.WriteLine("   FONT-FAMILY: Cambria, serif;")
txtstream.WriteLine("   FONT-SIZE: 12px;")
txtstream.WriteLine("   text-align: left;")
txtstream.WriteLine("   white-Space: nowrap='nowrap';")
txtstream.WriteLine("}")
txtstream.WriteLine("td")
txtstream.WriteLine("{")
txtstream.WriteLine("   COLOR: navy;")
txtstream.WriteLine("   BACKGROUND-COLOR: #eeeeee;")
txtstream.WriteLine("   FONT-FAMILY: Cambria, serif;")
txtstream.WriteLine("   FONT-SIZE: 12px;")
txtstream.WriteLine("   text-align: left;")
txtstream.WriteLine("   white-Space: nowrap='nowrap';")
txtstream.WriteLine("}")
txtstream.WriteLine("</style>")
txtstream.WriteLine("<body>")
txtstream.WriteLine("<table colspacing=""3"" colpadding=""3"">")


For x As Integer = 0 to rs.Fields.count-1
txtstream.WriteLine("<tr><th align='left' nowrap='true'>" +
col.Caption + "</th>")
txtstream.WriteLine("<xsl:for-each select=""data/Products""><td
align='left' nowrap='true'><xsl:value-of select=""" + col.Caption +
"""/></td></xsl:for-each></tr>")
next
txtstream.WriteLine("</table>")
txtstream.WriteLine("</body>")
txtstream.WriteLine("</html>")
txtstream.WriteLine("</xsl:template>")
txtstream.WriteLine("</xsl:stylesheet>")
```

```
txtstream.Close()
```

Tables

Single Line Horizontal

```
Dim cnstr as String = ""
Dim strQuery as String = ""

Dim cn As System.Data.SQLClient.SQLClientConnection  = new
System.Data.SQLClient.SQLClientConnection(cnstr)
cn.Open()

Dim cmd As System.Data.SQLClient.SQLClientCommand  = new
System.Data.SQLClient.SQLClientCommand()
cmd.Connection = cn
cmd.CommandType = 1
cmd.CommandText = strQuery
cmd.ExecuteNonquery()

Dim da As System.Data.SQLClient.SQLClientDataAdapter  = new
System.Data.SQLClient.SQLClientDataAdapter(cmd)

Dim dt as new System.Data.DataTable
da.Fill(dt)

Dim dv as System.Data.DataView = dt.DefaultView

Dim ws As Object  = CreateObject("WScript.Shell")
Dim fso As Object  = CreateObject("Scripting.FileSystemObject")
Dim txtstream as Object  = fso.OpenTextFile(ws.CurrentDirectory +
"\Products.xsl", 2, true, -2)
txtstream.WriteLine("<?xml version='1.0' encoding='UTF-8'?>")
txtstream.WriteLine("<xsl:stylesheet version='1.0'
xmlns:xsl='http://www.w3.org/1999/XSL/Transform'>")
```

```
txtstream.WriteLine("<xsl:template match=""/"">")
txtstream.WriteLine("<html>")
txtstream.WriteLine("<head>")
txtstream.WriteLine("<title>Products</title>")
txtstream.WriteLine("</head>")
txtstream.WriteLine("<style type='text/css'>")
txtstream.WriteLine("th")
txtstream.WriteLine(" {")
txtstream.WriteLine("    COLOR: darkred;")
txtstream.WriteLine("    BACKGROUND-COLOR: #eeeeee;")
txtstream.WriteLine("    FONT-FAMILY: Cambria, serif;")
txtstream.WriteLine("    FONT-SIZE: 12px;")
txtstream.WriteLine("    text-align: left;")
txtstream.WriteLine("    white-Space: nowrap='nowrap';")
txtstream.WriteLine("}")
txtstream.WriteLine("td")
txtstream.WriteLine(" {")
txtstream.WriteLine("    COLOR: navy;")
txtstream.WriteLine("    BACKGROUND-COLOR: #eeeeee;")
txtstream.WriteLine("    FONT-FAMILY: Cambria, serif;")
txtstream.WriteLine("    FONT-SIZE: 12px;")
txtstream.WriteLine("    text-align: left;")
txtstream.WriteLine("    white-Space: nowrap='nowrap';")
txtstream.WriteLine("}")
txtstream.WriteLine("</style>")
txtstream.WriteLine("<body>")
txtstream.WriteLine("<table style='border:Double;border-
width:1px;border-color:navy;' rules='all' frames='both' cellpadding='2'
cellspacing='2'>")


txtstream.WriteLine("<tr>")
For x As Integer = 0 to rs.Fields.count-1
txtstream.WriteLine("<th align='left' nowrap='true'>" + col.Caption +
"</th>")
next
txtstream.WriteLine("</tr>")
```

```
txtstream.WriteLine("<tr>")
For x As Integer = 0 to rs.Fields.count-1
txtstream.WriteLine("<td><xsl:value-of select=""data/Products/" +
col.Caption  + """/></td>")
next
txtstream.WriteLine("</tr>")
txtstream.WriteLine("</table>")
txtstream.WriteLine("</body>")
txtstream.WriteLine("</html>")
txtstream.WriteLine("</xsl:template>")
txtstream.WriteLine("</xsl:stylesheet>")
txtstream.Close()
```

Multi Line Horizontal

```
Dim cnstr as String = ""
Dim strQuery as String = ""

Dim cn As System.Data.SQLClient.SQLClientConnection  = new
System.Data.SQLClient.SQLClientConnection(cnstr)
cn.Open()

Dim cmd As System.Data.SQLClient.SQLClientCommand  = new
System.Data.SQLClient.SQLClientCommand()
cmd.Connection = cn
cmd.CommandType = 1
cmd.CommandText = strQuery
cmd.ExecuteNonquery()

Dim da As System.Data.SQLClient.SQLClientDataAdapter  = new
System.Data.SQLClient.SQLClientDataAdapter(cmd)

Dim dt as new System.Data.DataTable
da.Fill(dt)
```

```
Dim dv as System.Data.DataView = dt.DefaultView

Dim ws As Object  = CreateObject("WScript.Shell")
Dim fso As Object  = CreateObject("Scripting.FileSystemObject")
Dim txtstream as Object  = fso.OpenTextFile(ws.CurrentDirectory +
"\Products.xsl", 2, true, -2)
txtstream.WriteLine("<?xml version='1.0' encoding='UTF-8'?>")
txtstream.WriteLine("<xsl:stylesheet version='1.0'
xmlns:xsl='http://www.w3.org/1999/XSL/Transform'>")
txtstream.WriteLine("<xsl:template match=""/"">")
txtstream.WriteLine("<html>")
txtstream.WriteLine("<head>")
txtstream.WriteLine("<title>Products</title>")
txtstream.WriteLine("</head>")
txtstream.WriteLine("<style type='text/css'>")
txtstream.WriteLine("th")
txtstream.WriteLine(" {")
txtstream.WriteLine("    COLOR: darkred;")
txtstream.WriteLine("    BACKGROUND-COLOR: #eeeeee;")
txtstream.WriteLine("    FONT-FAMILY: Cambria, serif;")
txtstream.WriteLine("    FONT-SIZE: 12px;")
txtstream.WriteLine("    text-align: left;")
txtstream.WriteLine("    white-Space: nowrap='nowrap';")
txtstream.WriteLine("}")
txtstream.WriteLine("td")
txtstream.WriteLine(" {")
txtstream.WriteLine("    COLOR: navy;")
txtstream.WriteLine("    BACKGROUND-COLOR: #eeeeee;")
txtstream.WriteLine("    FONT-FAMILY: Cambria, serif;")
txtstream.WriteLine("    FONT-SIZE: 12px;")
txtstream.WriteLine("    text-align: left;")
txtstream.WriteLine("    white-Space: nowrap='nowrap';")
txtstream.WriteLine("}")
txtstream.WriteLine("</style>")
txtstream.WriteLine("<body>")
```

```
txtstream.WriteLine("<table style='border:Double;border-
width:1px;border-color:navy;' rules='all' frames='both' cellpadding='2'
cellspacing='2'>")


txtstream.WriteLine("<tr>")
For x As Integer = 0 to rs.Fields.count-1
txtstream.WriteLine("<th>" + col.Caption + "</th>")
next
txtstream.WriteLine("</tr>")
txtstream.WriteLine("<xsl:for-each select=""data/Products"">")
txtstream.WriteLine("<tr>")
For x As Integer = 0 to rs.Fields.count-1
txtstream.WriteLine("<td><xsl:value-of select="" " + col.Caption + "
""/></td>")
txtstream.WriteLine("<td><xsl:value-of select=""" + col.Caption  +
"""/></td>")
next
txtstream.WriteLine("</tr>")
txtstream.WriteLine("</xsl:for-each>")
txtstream.WriteLine("</table>")
txtstream.WriteLine("</body>")
txtstream.WriteLine("</html>")
txtstream.WriteLine("</xsl:template>")
txtstream.WriteLine("</xsl:stylesheet>")
txtstream.Close()
```

Single Line Vertical

```
Dim cnstr as String = ""
Dim strQuery as String = ""

Dim cn As System.Data.SQLClient.SQLClientConnection  = new
System.Data.SQLClient.SQLClientConnection(cnstr)
cn.Open()
```

```
Dim cmd As System.Data.SQLClient.SQLClientCommand = new
System.Data.SQLClient.SQLClientCommand()
cmd.Connection = cn
cmd.CommandType = 1
cmd.CommandText = strQuery
cmd.ExecuteNonquery()

Dim da As System.Data.SQLClient.SQLClientDataAdapter = new
System.Data.SQLClient.SQLClientDataAdapter(cmd)

Dim dt as new System.Data.DataTable
da.Fill(dt)

Dim dv as System.Data.DataView = dt.DefaultView

Dim ws As Object = CreateObject("WScript.Shell")
Dim fso As Object = CreateObject("Scripting.FileSystemObject")
Dim txtstream as Object = fso.OpenTextFile(ws.CurrentDirectory +
"\Products.xsl", 2, true, -2)
txtstream.WriteLine("<?xml version='1.0' encoding='UTF-8'?>")
txtstream.WriteLine("<xsl:stylesheet version='1.0'
xmlns:xsl='http://www.w3.org/1999/XSL/Transform'>")
txtstream.WriteLine("<xsl:template match=""""/"""">")
txtstream.WriteLine("<html>")
txtstream.WriteLine("<head>")
txtstream.WriteLine("<title>Products</title>")
txtstream.WriteLine("</head>")
txtstream.WriteLine("<style type='text/css'>")
txtstream.WriteLine("th")
txtstream.WriteLine(" {")
txtstream.WriteLine("    COLOR: darkred;")
txtstream.WriteLine("    BACKGROUND-COLOR: #eeeeee;")
txtstream.WriteLine("    FONT-FAMILY: Cambria, serif;")
txtstream.WriteLine("    FONT-SIZE: 12px;")
txtstream.WriteLine("    text-align: left;")
txtstream.WriteLine("    white-Space: nowrap='nowrap';")
```

```
txtstream.WriteLine("}")
txtstream.WriteLine("td")
txtstream.WriteLine(" {")
txtstream.WriteLine("    COLOR: navy;")
txtstream.WriteLine("    BACKGROUND-COLOR: #eeeeee;")
txtstream.WriteLine("    FONT-FAMILY: Cambria, serif;")
txtstream.WriteLine("    FONT-SIZE: 12px;")
txtstream.WriteLine("    text-align: left;")
txtstream.WriteLine("    white-Space: nowrap='nowrap';")
txtstream.WriteLine("}")
txtstream.WriteLine("</style>")
txtstream.WriteLine("<body>")
txtstream.WriteLine("<table style='border:Double;border-
width:1px;border-color:navy;' rules='all' frames='both' cellpadding='2'
cellspacing='2'>")


For x As Integer = 0 to rs.Fields.count-1
txtstream.WriteLine("<tr><th>" + col.Caption + "</th>")
txtstream.WriteLine("<td><xsl:value-of select=""data/Products/" +
col.Caption  + """/></td></tr>")
next
txtstream.WriteLine("</table>")
txtstream.WriteLine("</body>")
txtstream.WriteLine("</html>")
txtstream.WriteLine("</xsl:template>")
txtstream.WriteLine("</xsl:stylesheet>")
txtstream.Close()
```

Multi Line Vertical

```
Dim cnstr as String = ""
```

```
Dim strQuery as String = ""

Dim cn As System.Data.SQLClient.SQLClientConnection  = new
System.Data.SQLClient.SQLClientConnection(cnstr)
cn.Open()

Dim cmd As System.Data.SQLClient.SQLClientCommand  = new
System.Data.SQLClient.SQLClientCommand()
cmd.Connection = cn
cmd.CommandType = 1
cmd.CommandText = strQuery
cmd.ExecuteNonquery()

Dim da As System.Data.SQLClient.SQLClientDataAdapter  = new
System.Data.SQLClient.SQLClientDataAdapter(cmd)

Dim dt as new System.Data.DataTable
da.Fill(dt)

Dim dv as System.Data.DataView = dt.DefaultView

Dim ws As Object  = CreateObject("WScript.Shell")
Dim fso As Object  = CreateObject("Scripting.FileSystemObject")
Dim txtstream as Object  = fso.OpenTextFile(ws.CurrentDirectory +
"\Products.xsl", 2, true, -2)
txtstream.WriteLine("<?xml version='1.0' encoding='UTF-8'?>")
txtstream.WriteLine("<xsl:stylesheet version='1.0'
xmlns:xsl='http://www.w3.org/1999/XSL/Transform'>")
txtstream.WriteLine("<xsl:template match=''/''>")
txtstream.WriteLine("<html>")
txtstream.WriteLine("<head>")
txtstream.WriteLine("<title>Products</title>")
txtstream.WriteLine("</head>")
txtstream.WriteLine("<style type='text/css'>")
txtstream.WriteLine("th")
txtstream.WriteLine(" {")
txtstream.WriteLine("   COLOR: darkred;")
```

```
txtstream.WriteLine("    BACKGROUND-COLOR: #eeeeee;")
txtstream.WriteLine("    FONT-FAMILY: Cambria, serif;")
txtstream.WriteLine("    FONT-SIZE: 12px;")
txtstream.WriteLine("    text-align: left;")
txtstream.WriteLine("    white-Space: nowrap='nowrap';")
txtstream.WriteLine("}")
txtstream.WriteLine("td")
txtstream.WriteLine(" {")
txtstream.WriteLine("    COLOR: navy;")
txtstream.WriteLine("    BACKGROUND-COLOR: #eeeeee;")
txtstream.WriteLine("    FONT-FAMILY: Cambria, serif;")
txtstream.WriteLine("    FONT-SIZE: 12px;")
txtstream.WriteLine("    text-align: left;")
txtstream.WriteLine("    white-Space: nowrap='nowrap';")
txtstream.WriteLine("}")
txtstream.WriteLine("</style>")
txtstream.WriteLine("<body>")
txtstream.WriteLine("<table style='border:Double;border-
width:1px;border-color:navy;' rules='all' frames='both' cellpadding='2'
cellspacing='2'>")

For x As Integer = 0 to rs.Fields.count-1
txtstream.WriteLine("<tr><th align='left' nowrap='true'>" +
col.Caption + "</th>")
txtstream.WriteLine("<xsl:for-each select=""data/Products""><td
align='left' nowrap='true'><xsl:value-of select=""" + col.Caption +
"""/></td></xsl:for-each></tr>")
next
txtstream.WriteLine("</table>")
txtstream.WriteLine("</body>")
txtstream.WriteLine("</html>")
txtstream.WriteLine("</xsl:template>")
txtstream.WriteLine("</xsl:stylesheet>")
txtstream.Close()
```

Stylesheets
Some CSS Decorated Fuel for Thought

These are here for your consideration.

NONE

txtstream.WriteLine("<style type='text/css'>")

txtstream.WriteLine("th")

txtstream.WriteLine("")

txtstream.WriteLine("   COLOR: white;")

txtstream.WriteLine(" Next")

txtstream.WriteLine("td")

txtstream.WriteLine("")

txtstream.WriteLine("   COLOR: white;")

txtstream.WriteLine(" Next")

txtstream.WriteLine("</style>")

BLACK AND WHITE TEXT

txtstream.WriteLine("<style type='text/css'>")

txtstream.WriteLine("th")

txtstream.WriteLine("")

txtstream.WriteLine("   COLOR: white;")

txtstream.WriteLine("   BACKGROUND-COLOR: black;")

txtstream.WriteLine("   FONT-FAMILY: Cambria, serif;")

txtstream.WriteLine("   FONT-SIZE: 12px;")

txtstream.WriteLine("   text-align: left;")

txtstream.WriteLine("   white-Space: nowrap;")

txtstream.WriteLine(" Next")

txtstream.WriteLine("td")

txtstream.WriteLine("")

txtstream.WriteLine("   COLOR: white;")

txtstream.WriteLine("   BACKGROUND-COLOR: black;")

txtstream.WriteLine("   FONT-FAMILY: Cambria, serif;")

txtstream.WriteLine("   FONT-SIZE: 12px;")

txtstream.WriteLine("   text-align: left;")

txtstream.WriteLine("   white-Space: nowrap;")

txtstream.WriteLine(" Next")

txtstream.WriteLine("div")

txtstream.WriteLine("")

txtstream.WriteLine("   COLOR: white;")

txtstream.WriteLine("   BACKGROUND-COLOR: black;")

```
txtstream.WriteLine("    FONT-FAMILY: Cambria, serif;")
txtstream.WriteLine("    FONT-SIZE: 10px;")
txtstream.WriteLine("    text-align: left;")
txtstream.WriteLine("    white-Space: nowrap;")
txtstream.WriteLine(" Next")
txtstream.WriteLine("span")
txtstream.WriteLine("'")
txtstream.WriteLine("    COLOR: white;")
txtstream.WriteLine("    BACKGROUND-COLOR: black;")
txtstream.WriteLine("    FONT-FAMILY: Cambria, serif;")
txtstream.WriteLine("    FONT-SIZE: 10px;")
txtstream.WriteLine("    text-align: left;")
txtstream.WriteLine("    white-Space: nowrap;")
txtstream.WriteLine("    display:inline-block;")
txtstream.WriteLine("    width: 100%;")
txtstream.WriteLine(" Next")
txtstream.WriteLine("textarea")
txtstream.WriteLine("'")
txtstream.WriteLine("    COLOR: white;")
txtstream.WriteLine("    BACKGROUND-COLOR: black;")
txtstream.WriteLine("    FONT-FAMILY: Cambria, serif;")
txtstream.WriteLine("    FONT-SIZE: 10px;")
txtstream.WriteLine("    text-align: left;")
txtstream.WriteLine("    white-Space: nowrap;")
txtstream.WriteLine("    width: 100%;")
```

```
txtstream.WriteLine(" Next")
txtstream.WriteLine("select")
txtstream.WriteLine("{")
txtstream.WriteLine("    COLOR: white;")
txtstream.WriteLine("    BACKGROUND-COLOR: black;")
txtstream.WriteLine("    FONT-FAMILY: Cambria, serif;")
txtstream.WriteLine("    FONT-SIZE: 10px;")
txtstream.WriteLine("    text-align: left;")
txtstream.WriteLine("    white-Space: nowrap;")
txtstream.WriteLine("    width: 100%;")
txtstream.WriteLine(" Next")
txtstream.WriteLine("input")
txtstream.WriteLine("{")
txtstream.WriteLine("    COLOR: white;")
txtstream.WriteLine("    BACKGROUND-COLOR: black;")
txtstream.WriteLine("    FONT-FAMILY: Cambria, serif;")
txtstream.WriteLine("    FONT-SIZE: 12px;")
txtstream.WriteLine("    text-align: left;")
txtstream.WriteLine("    display:table-cell;")
txtstream.WriteLine("    white-Space: nowrap;")
txtstream.WriteLine(" Next")
txtstream.WriteLine("h1 {")
txtstream.WriteLine("color: antiquewhite;")
txtstream.WriteLine("text-shadow: 1px 1px 1px black;")
txtstream.WriteLine("padding: 3px;")
```

txtstream.WriteLine("text-align: center;")

txtstream.WriteLine("box-shadow: inSet 2px 2px 5px rgba(0,0,0,0.5), inSet -2px -2px 5px rgba(255,255,255,0.5);")

txtstream.WriteLine(" Next")

txtstream.WriteLine("</style>")

COLORED TEXT

txtstream.WriteLine("<style type='text/css'>")

txtstream.WriteLine("th")

txtstream.WriteLine("")

txtstream.WriteLine("   COLOR: darkred;")

txtstream.WriteLine("   BACKGROUND-COLOR: #eeeeee;")

txtstream.WriteLine("   FONT-FAMILY: Cambria, serif;")

txtstream.WriteLine("   FONT-SIZE: 12px;")

txtstream.WriteLine("   text-align: left;")

txtstream.WriteLine("   white-Space: nowrap;")

txtstream.WriteLine(" Next")

txtstream.WriteLine("td")

txtstream.WriteLine("")

txtstream.WriteLine("   COLOR: navy;")

txtstream.WriteLine("   BACKGROUND-COLOR: #eeeeee;")

txtstream.WriteLine("   FONT-FAMILY: Cambria, serif;")

txtstream.WriteLine("   FONT-SIZE: 12px;")

txtstream.WriteLine("   text-align: left;")

txtstream.WriteLine("   white-Space: nowrap;")

```
txtstream.WriteLine(" Next")
txtstream.WriteLine("div")
txtstream.WriteLine("'")
txtstream.WriteLine("    COLOR: white;")
txtstream.WriteLine("    BACKGROUND-COLOR: navy;")
txtstream.WriteLine("    FONT-FAMILY: Cambria, serif;")
txtstream.WriteLine("    FONT-SIZE: 10px;")
txtstream.WriteLine("    text-align: left;")
txtstream.WriteLine("    white-Space: nowrap;")
txtstream.WriteLine(" Next")
txtstream.WriteLine("span")
txtstream.WriteLine("'")
txtstream.WriteLine("    COLOR: white;")
txtstream.WriteLine("    BACKGROUND-COLOR: navy;")
txtstream.WriteLine("    FONT-FAMILY: Cambria, serif;")
txtstream.WriteLine("    FONT-SIZE: 10px;")
txtstream.WriteLine("    text-align: left;")
txtstream.WriteLine("    white-Space: nowrap;")
txtstream.WriteLine("    display:inline-block;")
txtstream.WriteLine("    width: 100%;")
txtstream.WriteLine(" Next")
txtstream.WriteLine("textarea")
txtstream.WriteLine("'")
txtstream.WriteLine("    COLOR: white;")
txtstream.WriteLine("    BACKGROUND-COLOR: navy;")
```

```
txtstream.WriteLine("    FONT-FAMILY: Cambria, serif;")
txtstream.WriteLine("    FONT-SIZE: 10px;")
txtstream.WriteLine("    text-align: left;")
txtstream.WriteLine("    white-Space: nowrap;")
txtstream.WriteLine("    width: 100%;")
txtstream.WriteLine(" Next")
txtstream.WriteLine("select")
txtstream.WriteLine("'")
txtstream.WriteLine("    COLOR: white;")
txtstream.WriteLine("    BACKGROUND-COLOR: navy;")
txtstream.WriteLine("    FONT-FAMILY: Cambria, serif;")
txtstream.WriteLine("    FONT-SIZE: 10px;")
txtstream.WriteLine("    text-align: left;")
txtstream.WriteLine("    white-Space: nowrap;")
txtstream.WriteLine("    width: 100%;")
txtstream.WriteLine(" Next")
txtstream.WriteLine("input")
txtstream.WriteLine("'")
txtstream.WriteLine("    COLOR: white;")
txtstream.WriteLine("    BACKGROUND-COLOR: navy;")
txtstream.WriteLine("    FONT-FAMILY: Cambria, serif;")
txtstream.WriteLine("    FONT-SIZE: 12px;")
txtstream.WriteLine("    text-align: left;")
txtstream.WriteLine("    display:table-cell;")
txtstream.WriteLine("    white-Space: nowrap;")
```

```
txtstream.WriteLine(" Next")

txtstream.WriteLine("h1 ")

txtstream.WriteLine("color: antiquewhite;")

txtstream.WriteLine("text-shadow: 1px 1px 1px black;")

txtstream.WriteLine("padding: 3px;")

txtstream.WriteLine("text-align: center;")

txtstream.WriteLine("box-shadow: inSet 2px 2px 5px rgba(0,0,0,0.5),
inSet -2px -2px 5px rgba(255,255,255,0.5);")

txtstream.WriteLine(" Next")

txtstream.WriteLine("</style>")
```

OSCILLATING ROW COLORS

```
txtstream.WriteLine("<style>")

txtstream.WriteLine("th")

txtstream.WriteLine("")

txtstream.WriteLine("    COLOR: white;")

txtstream.WriteLine("    BACKGROUND-COLOR: navy;")

txtstream.WriteLine("    FONT-FAMILY: Cambria, serif;")

txtstream.WriteLine("    FONT-SIZE: 12px;")

txtstream.WriteLine("    text-align: left;")

txtstream.WriteLine("    white-Space: nowrap;")

txtstream.WriteLine(" Next")
```

txtstream.WriteLine("td")

txtstream.WriteLine("'")

txtstream.WriteLine("   COLOR: navy;")

txtstream.WriteLine("   FONT-FAMILY: Cambria, serif;")

txtstream.WriteLine("   FONT-SIZE: 12px;")

txtstream.WriteLine("   text-align: left;")

txtstream.WriteLine("   white-Space: nowrap;")

txtstream.WriteLine(" Next")

txtstream.WriteLine("div")

txtstream.WriteLine("'")

txtstream.WriteLine("   COLOR: navy;")

txtstream.WriteLine("   FONT-FAMILY: Cambria, serif;")

txtstream.WriteLine("   FONT-SIZE: 12px;")

txtstream.WriteLine("   text-align: left;")

txtstream.WriteLine("   white-Space: nowrap;")

txtstream.WriteLine(" Next")

txtstream.WriteLine("span")

txtstream.WriteLine("'")

txtstream.WriteLine("   COLOR: navy;")

txtstream.WriteLine("   FONT-FAMILY: Cambria, serif;")

txtstream.WriteLine("   FONT-SIZE: 12px;")

txtstream.WriteLine("   text-align: left;")

txtstream.WriteLine("   white-Space: nowrap;")

txtstream.WriteLine("   width: 100%;")

txtstream.WriteLine(" Next")

```
txtstream.WriteLine("textarea")
txtstream.WriteLine("'")
txtstream.WriteLine("   COLOR: navy;")
txtstream.WriteLine("   FONT-FAMILY: Cambria, serif;")
txtstream.WriteLine("   FONT-SIZE: 12px;")
txtstream.WriteLine("   text-align: left;")
txtstream.WriteLine("   white-Space: nowrap;")
txtstream.WriteLine("   display:inline-block;")
txtstream.WriteLine("   width: 100%;")
txtstream.WriteLine(" Next")
txtstream.WriteLine("select")
txtstream.WriteLine("'")
txtstream.WriteLine("   COLOR: navy;")
txtstream.WriteLine("   FONT-FAMILY: Cambria, serif;")
txtstream.WriteLine("   FONT-SIZE: 10px;")
txtstream.WriteLine("   text-align: left;")
txtstream.WriteLine("   white-Space: nowrap;")
txtstream.WriteLine("   display:inline-block;")
txtstream.WriteLine("   width: 100%;")
txtstream.WriteLine(" Next")
txtstream.WriteLine("input")
txtstream.WriteLine("'")
txtstream.WriteLine("   COLOR: navy;")
txtstream.WriteLine("   FONT-FAMILY: Cambria, serif;")
txtstream.WriteLine("   FONT-SIZE: 12px;")
```

```
txtstream.WriteLine("     text-align: left;")

txtstream.WriteLine("     display:table-cell;")

txtstream.WriteLine("     white-Space: nowrap;")

txtstream.WriteLine(" Next")

txtstream.WriteLine("h1 ")

txtstream.WriteLine("color: antiquewhite;")

txtstream.WriteLine("text-shadow: 1px 1px 1px black;")

txtstream.WriteLine("padding: 3px;")

txtstream.WriteLine("text-align: center;")

txtstream.WriteLine("box-shadow: inSet 2px 2px 5px rgba(0,0,0,0.5),
inSet -2px -2px 5px rgba(255,255,255,0.5);")

txtstream.WriteLine(" Next")

txtstream.WriteLine("tr:nth-child(even)background-color:#f2f2f2;
Next")

txtstream.WriteLine("tr:nth-child(odd)background-color:#cccccc;
color:#f2f2f2; Next")

txtstream.WriteLine("</style>")
```

GHOST DECORATED

```
txtstream.WriteLine("<style type='text/css'>")

txtstream.WriteLine("th")

txtstream.WriteLine("")

txtstream.WriteLine("     COLOR: black;")

txtstream.WriteLine("     BACKGROUND-COLOR: white;")
```

```
txtstream.WriteLine("    FONT-FAMILY: Cambria, serif;")
txtstream.WriteLine("    FONT-SIZE: 12px;")
txtstream.WriteLine("    text-align: left;")
txtstream.WriteLine("    white-Space: nowrap;")
txtstream.WriteLine(" Next")
txtstream.WriteLine("td")
txtstream.WriteLine("")
txtstream.WriteLine("    COLOR: black;")
txtstream.WriteLine("    BACKGROUND-COLOR: white;")
txtstream.WriteLine("    FONT-FAMILY: Cambria, serif;")
txtstream.WriteLine("    FONT-SIZE: 12px;")
txtstream.WriteLine("    text-align: left;")
txtstream.WriteLine("    white-Space: nowrap;")
txtstream.WriteLine(" Next")
txtstream.WriteLine("div")
txtstream.WriteLine("")
txtstream.WriteLine("    COLOR: black;")
txtstream.WriteLine("    BACKGROUND-COLOR: white;")
txtstream.WriteLine("    FONT-FAMILY: Cambria, serif;")
txtstream.WriteLine("    FONT-SIZE: 10px;")
txtstream.WriteLine("    text-align: left;")
txtstream.WriteLine("    white-Space: nowrap;")
txtstream.WriteLine(" Next")
txtstream.WriteLine("span")
txtstream.WriteLine("")
```

```
txtstream.WriteLine("    COLOR: black;")
txtstream.WriteLine("    BACKGROUND-COLOR: white;")
txtstream.WriteLine("    FONT-FAMILY: Cambria, serif;")
txtstream.WriteLine("    FONT-SIZE: 10px;")
txtstream.WriteLine("    text-align: left;")
txtstream.WriteLine("    white-Space: nowrap;")
txtstream.WriteLine("    display:inline-block;")
txtstream.WriteLine("    width: 100%;")
txtstream.WriteLine(" Next")
txtstream.WriteLine("textarea")
txtstream.WriteLine("'")
txtstream.WriteLine("    COLOR: black;")
txtstream.WriteLine("    BACKGROUND-COLOR: white;")
txtstream.WriteLine("    FONT-FAMILY: Cambria, serif;")
txtstream.WriteLine("    FONT-SIZE: 10px;")
txtstream.WriteLine("    text-align: left;")
txtstream.WriteLine("    white-Space: nowrap;")
txtstream.WriteLine("    width: 100%;")
txtstream.WriteLine(" Next")
txtstream.WriteLine("select")
txtstream.WriteLine("'")
txtstream.WriteLine("    COLOR: black;")
txtstream.WriteLine("    BACKGROUND-COLOR: white;")
txtstream.WriteLine("    FONT-FAMILY: Cambria, serif;")
txtstream.WriteLine("    FONT-SIZE: 10px;")
```

```
txtstream.WriteLine("    text-align: left;")
txtstream.WriteLine("    white-Space: nowrap;")
txtstream.WriteLine("    width: 100%;")
txtstream.WriteLine(" Next")
txtstream.WriteLine("input")
txtstream.WriteLine("'")
txtstream.WriteLine("    COLOR: black;")
txtstream.WriteLine("    BACKGROUND-COLOR: white;")
txtstream.WriteLine("    FONT-FAMILY: Cambria, serif;")
txtstream.WriteLine("    FONT-SIZE: 12px;")
txtstream.WriteLine("    text-align: left;")
txtstream.WriteLine("    display:table-cell;")
txtstream.WriteLine("    white-Space: nowrap;")
txtstream.WriteLine(" Next")
txtstream.WriteLine("h1 '")
txtstream.WriteLine("color: antiquewhite;")
txtstream.WriteLine("text-shadow: 1px 1px 1px black;")
txtstream.WriteLine("padding: 3px;")
txtstream.WriteLine("text-align: center;")
txtstream.WriteLine("box-shadow: inSet 2px 2px 5px rgba(0,0,0,0.5),
inSet -2px -2px 5px rgba(255,255,255,0.5);")
txtstream.WriteLine(" Next")
txtstream.WriteLine("</style>'")
```

```
txtstream.WriteLine("<style type='text/css'>")
txtstream.WriteLine("body")
txtstream.WriteLine("")
txtstream.WriteLine("    PADDING-RIGHT: 0px;")
txtstream.WriteLine("    PADDING-LEFT: 0px;")
txtstream.WriteLine("    PADDING-BOTTOM: 0px;")
txtstream.WriteLine("    MARGIN: 0px;")
txtstream.WriteLine("    COLOR: #333;")
txtstream.WriteLine("    PADDING-TOP: 0px;")
txtstream.WriteLine("    FONT-FAMILY: verdana, arial, helvetica, sans-serif;")
txtstream.WriteLine(" Next")
txtstream.WriteLine("table")
txtstream.WriteLine("")
txtstream.WriteLine("    BORDER-RIGHT: #999999 3px solid;")
txtstream.WriteLine("    PADDING-RIGHT: 6px;")
txtstream.WriteLine("    PADDING-LEFT: 6px;")
txtstream.WriteLine("    FONT-WEIGHT: Bold;")
txtstream.WriteLine("    FONT-SIZE: 14px;")
txtstream.WriteLine("    PADDING-BOTTOM: 6px;")
txtstream.WriteLine("    COLOR: Peru;")
txtstream.WriteLine("    LINE-HEIGHT: 14px;")
```

```
txtstream.WriteLine("    PADDING-TOP: 6px;")
txtstream.WriteLine("    BORDER-BOTTOM: #999 1px solid;")
txtstream.WriteLine("    BACKGROUND-COLOR: #eeeeee;")
txtstream.WriteLine("    FONT-FAMILY: verdana, arial, helvetica, sans-serif;")
txtstream.WriteLine("    FONT-SIZE: 12px;")
txtstream.WriteLine(" Next")
txtstream.WriteLine("th")
txtstream.WriteLine("'")
txtstream.WriteLine("    BORDER-RIGHT: #999999 3px solid;")
txtstream.WriteLine("    PADDING-RIGHT: 6px;")
txtstream.WriteLine("    PADDING-LEFT: 6px;")
txtstream.WriteLine("    FONT-WEIGHT: Bold;")
txtstream.WriteLine("    FONT-SIZE: 14px;")
txtstream.WriteLine("    PADDING-BOTTOM: 6px;")
txtstream.WriteLine("    COLOR: darkred;")
txtstream.WriteLine("    LINE-HEIGHT: 14px;")
txtstream.WriteLine("    PADDING-TOP: 6px;")
txtstream.WriteLine("    BORDER-BOTTOM: #999 1px solid;")
txtstream.WriteLine("    BACKGROUND-COLOR: #eeeeee;")
txtstream.WriteLine("    FONT-FAMILY: Cambria, serif;")
txtstream.WriteLine("    FONT-SIZE: 12px;")
txtstream.WriteLine("    text-align: left;")
txtstream.WriteLine("    white-Space: nowrap;")
txtstream.WriteLine(" Next")
```

```
txtstream.WriteLine(".th")
txtstream.WriteLine("'")
txtstream.WriteLine("    BORDER-RIGHT: #999999 2px solid;")
txtstream.WriteLine("    PADDING-RIGHT: 6px;")
txtstream.WriteLine("    PADDING-LEFT: 6px;")
txtstream.WriteLine("    FONT-WEIGHT: Bold;")
txtstream.WriteLine("    PADDING-BOTTOM: 6px;")
txtstream.WriteLine("    COLOR: black;")
txtstream.WriteLine("    PADDING-TOP: 6px;")
txtstream.WriteLine("    BORDER-BOTTOM: #999 2px solid;")
txtstream.WriteLine("    BACKGROUND-COLOR: #eeeeee;")
txtstream.WriteLine("    FONT-FAMILY: Cambria, serif;")
txtstream.WriteLine("    FONT-SIZE: 10px;")
txtstream.WriteLine("    text-align: right;")
txtstream.WriteLine("    white-Space: nowrap;")
txtstream.WriteLine(" Next")
txtstream.WriteLine("td")
txtstream.WriteLine("'")
txtstream.WriteLine("    BORDER-RIGHT: #999999 3px solid;")
txtstream.WriteLine("    PADDING-RIGHT: 6px;")
txtstream.WriteLine("    PADDING-LEFT: 6px;")
txtstream.WriteLine("    FONT-WEIGHT: Normal;")
txtstream.WriteLine("    PADDING-BOTTOM: 6px;")
txtstream.WriteLine("    COLOR: navy;")
txtstream.WriteLine("    LINE-HEIGHT: 14px;")
```

```
txtstream.WriteLine("    PADDING-TOP: 6px;")

txtstream.WriteLine("    BORDER-BOTTOM: #999 1px solid;")

txtstream.WriteLine("    BACKGROUND-COLOR: #eeeeee;")

txtstream.WriteLine("    FONT-FAMILY: Cambria, serif;")

txtstream.WriteLine("    FONT-SIZE: 12px;")

txtstream.WriteLine("    text-align: left;")

txtstream.WriteLine("    white-Space: nowrap;")

txtstream.WriteLine(" Next")

txtstream.WriteLine("div")

txtstream.WriteLine("'")

txtstream.WriteLine("    BORDER-RIGHT: #999999 3px solid;")

txtstream.WriteLine("    PADDING-RIGHT: 6px;")

txtstream.WriteLine("    PADDING-LEFT: 6px;")

txtstream.WriteLine("    FONT-WEIGHT: Normal;")

txtstream.WriteLine("    PADDING-BOTTOM: 6px;")

txtstream.WriteLine("    COLOR: white;")

txtstream.WriteLine("    PADDING-TOP: 6px;")

txtstream.WriteLine("    BORDER-BOTTOM: #999 1px solid;")

txtstream.WriteLine("    BACKGROUND-COLOR: navy;")

txtstream.WriteLine("    FONT-FAMILY: Cambria, serif;")

txtstream.WriteLine("    FONT-SIZE: 10px;")

txtstream.WriteLine("    text-align: left;")

txtstream.WriteLine("    white-Space: nowrap;")

txtstream.WriteLine(" Next")

txtstream.WriteLine("span")
```

```
txtstream.WriteLine(""")
txtstream.WriteLine("    BORDER-RIGHT: #999999 3px solid;")
txtstream.WriteLine("    PADDING-RIGHT: 3px;")
txtstream.WriteLine("    PADDING-LEFT: 3px;")
txtstream.WriteLine("    FONT-WEIGHT: Normal;")
txtstream.WriteLine("    PADDING-BOTTOM: 3px;")
txtstream.WriteLine("    COLOR: white;")
txtstream.WriteLine("    PADDING-TOP: 3px;")
txtstream.WriteLine("    BORDER-BOTTOM: #999 1px solid;")
txtstream.WriteLine("    BACKGROUND-COLOR: navy;")
txtstream.WriteLine("    FONT-FAMILY: Cambria, serif;")
txtstream.WriteLine("    FONT-SIZE: 10px;")
txtstream.WriteLine("    text-align: left;")
txtstream.WriteLine("    white-Space: nowrap;")
txtstream.WriteLine("    display:inline-block;")
txtstream.WriteLine("    width: 100%;")
txtstream.WriteLine(" Next")
txtstream.WriteLine("textarea")
txtstream.WriteLine(""")
txtstream.WriteLine("    BORDER-RIGHT: #999999 3px solid;")
txtstream.WriteLine("    PADDING-RIGHT: 3px;")
txtstream.WriteLine("    PADDING-LEFT: 3px;")
txtstream.WriteLine("    FONT-WEIGHT: Normal;")
txtstream.WriteLine("    PADDING-BOTTOM: 3px;")
txtstream.WriteLine("    COLOR: white;")
```

```
txtstream.WriteLine("    PADDING-TOP: 3px;")
txtstream.WriteLine("    BORDER-BOTTOM: #999 1px solid;")
txtstream.WriteLine("    BACKGROUND-COLOR: navy;")
txtstream.WriteLine("    FONT-FAMILY: Cambria, serif;")
txtstream.WriteLine("    FONT-SIZE: 10px;")
txtstream.WriteLine("    text-align: left;")
txtstream.WriteLine("    white-Space: nowrap;")
txtstream.WriteLine("    width: 100%;")
txtstream.WriteLine(" Next")
txtstream.WriteLine("select")
txtstream.WriteLine("")
txtstream.WriteLine("    BORDER-RIGHT: #999999 3px solid;")
txtstream.WriteLine("    PADDING-RIGHT: 6px;")
txtstream.WriteLine("    PADDING-LEFT: 6px;")
txtstream.WriteLine("    FONT-WEIGHT: Normal;")
txtstream.WriteLine("    PADDING-BOTTOM: 6px;")
txtstream.WriteLine("    COLOR: white;")
txtstream.WriteLine("    PADDING-TOP: 6px;")
txtstream.WriteLine("    BORDER-BOTTOM: #999 1px solid;")
txtstream.WriteLine("    BACKGROUND-COLOR: navy;")
txtstream.WriteLine("    FONT-FAMILY: Cambria, serif;")
txtstream.WriteLine("    FONT-SIZE: 10px;")
txtstream.WriteLine("    text-align: left;")
txtstream.WriteLine("    white-Space: nowrap;")
txtstream.WriteLine("    width: 100%;")
```

```
txtstream.WriteLine(" Next")

txtstream.WriteLine("input")

txtstream.WriteLine("'")

txtstream.WriteLine("    BORDER-RIGHT: #999999 3px solid;")

txtstream.WriteLine("    PADDING-RIGHT: 3px;")

txtstream.WriteLine("    PADDING-LEFT: 3px;")

txtstream.WriteLine("    FONT-WEIGHT: Bold;")

txtstream.WriteLine("    PADDING-BOTTOM: 3px;")

txtstream.WriteLine("    COLOR: white;")

txtstream.WriteLine("    PADDING-TOP: 3px;")

txtstream.WriteLine("    BORDER-BOTTOM: #999 1px solid;")

txtstream.WriteLine("    BACKGROUND-COLOR: navy;")

txtstream.WriteLine("    FONT-FAMILY: Cambria, serif;")

txtstream.WriteLine("    FONT-SIZE: 12px;")

txtstream.WriteLine("    text-align: left;")

txtstream.WriteLine("    display:table-cell;")

txtstream.WriteLine("    white-Space: nowrap;")

txtstream.WriteLine("    width: 100%;")

txtstream.WriteLine(" Next")

txtstream.WriteLine("h1 '")

txtstream.WriteLine("color: antiquewhite;")

txtstream.WriteLine("text-shadow: 1px 1px 1px black;")

txtstream.WriteLine("padding: 3px;")

txtstream.WriteLine("text-align: center;")
```

txtstream.WriteLine("box-shadow: inSet 2px 2px 5px rgba(0,0,0,0.5), inSet -2px -2px 5px rgba(255,255,255,0.5);")

txtstream.WriteLine(" Next")

txtstream.WriteLine("</style>")

SHADOW BOX

txtstream.WriteLine("<style type='text/css'>")

txtstream.WriteLine("body")

txtstream.WriteLine("")

txtstream.WriteLine("   PADDING-RIGHT: 0px;")

txtstream.WriteLine("   PADDING-LEFT: 0px;")

txtstream.WriteLine("   PADDING-BOTTOM: 0px;")

txtstream.WriteLine("   MARGIN: 0px;")

txtstream.WriteLine("   COLOR: #333;")

txtstream.WriteLine("   PADDING-TOP: 0px;")

txtstream.WriteLine("   FONT-FAMILY: verdana, arial, helvetica, sans-serif;")

txtstream.WriteLine(" Next")

txtstream.WriteLine("table")

txtstream.WriteLine("")

txtstream.WriteLine("   BORDER-RIGHT: #999999 1px solid;")

txtstream.WriteLine("   PADDING-RIGHT: 1px;")

txtstream.WriteLine("   PADDING-LEFT: 1px;")

txtstream.WriteLine("   PADDING-BOTTOM: 1px;")

```
txtstream.WriteLine("    LINE-HEIGHT: 8px;")
txtstream.WriteLine("    PADDING-TOP: 1px;")
txtstream.WriteLine("    BORDER-BOTTOM: #999 1px solid;")
txtstream.WriteLine("    BACKGROUND-COLOR: #eeeeee;")
txtstream.WriteLine("
filter:progid:DXImageTransform.Microsoft.Shadow(color='silver',
Direction=135, Strength=16)")
txtstream.WriteLine(" Next")
txtstream.WriteLine("th")
txtstream.WriteLine("'")
txtstream.WriteLine("    BORDER-RIGHT: #999999 3px solid;")
txtstream.WriteLine("    PADDING-RIGHT: 6px;")
txtstream.WriteLine("    PADDING-LEFT: 6px;")
txtstream.WriteLine("    FONT-WEIGHT: Bold;")
txtstream.WriteLine("    FONT-SIZE: 14px;")
txtstream.WriteLine("    PADDING-BOTTOM: 6px;")
txtstream.WriteLine("    COLOR: darkred;")
txtstream.WriteLine("    LINE-HEIGHT: 14px;")
txtstream.WriteLine("    PADDING-TOP: 6px;")
txtstream.WriteLine("    BORDER-BOTTOM: #999 1px solid;")
txtstream.WriteLine("    BACKGROUND-COLOR: #eeeeee;")
txtstream.WriteLine("    FONT-FAMILY: Cambria, serif;")
txtstream.WriteLine("    FONT-SIZE: 12px;")
txtstream.WriteLine("    text-align: left;")
txtstream.WriteLine("    white-Space: nowrap;")
```

```
txtstream.WriteLine(" Next")
txtstream.WriteLine(".th")
txtstream.WriteLine("'")
txtstream.WriteLine("    BORDER-RIGHT: #999999 2px solid;")
txtstream.WriteLine("    PADDING-RIGHT: 6px;")
txtstream.WriteLine("    PADDING-LEFT: 6px;")
txtstream.WriteLine("    FONT-WEIGHT: Bold;")
txtstream.WriteLine("    PADDING-BOTTOM: 6px;")
txtstream.WriteLine("    COLOR: black;")
txtstream.WriteLine("    PADDING-TOP: 6px;")
txtstream.WriteLine("    BORDER-BOTTOM: #999 2px solid;")
txtstream.WriteLine("    BACKGROUND-COLOR: #eeeeee;")
txtstream.WriteLine("    FONT-FAMILY: Cambria, serif;")
txtstream.WriteLine("    FONT-SIZE: 10px;")
txtstream.WriteLine("    text-align: right;")
txtstream.WriteLine("    white-Space: nowrap;")
txtstream.WriteLine(" Next")
txtstream.WriteLine("td")
txtstream.WriteLine("'")
txtstream.WriteLine("    BORDER-RIGHT: #999999 3px solid;")
txtstream.WriteLine("    PADDING-RIGHT: 6px;")
txtstream.WriteLine("    PADDING-LEFT: 6px;")
txtstream.WriteLine("    FONT-WEIGHT: Normal;")
txtstream.WriteLine("    PADDING-BOTTOM: 6px;")
txtstream.WriteLine("    COLOR: navy;")
```

txtstream.WriteLine("   LINE-HEIGHT: 14px;")

txtstream.WriteLine("   PADDING-TOP: 6px;")

txtstream.WriteLine("   BORDER-BOTTOM: #999 1px solid;")

txtstream.WriteLine("   BACKGROUND-COLOR: #eeeeee;")

txtstream.WriteLine("   FONT-FAMILY: Cambria, serif;")

txtstream.WriteLine("   FONT-SIZE: 12px;")

txtstream.WriteLine("   text-align: left;")

txtstream.WriteLine("   white-Space: nowrap;")

txtstream.WriteLine(" Next")

txtstream.WriteLine("div")

txtstream.WriteLine("'")

txtstream.WriteLine("   BORDER-RIGHT: #999999 3px solid;")

txtstream.WriteLine("   PADDING-RIGHT: 6px;")

txtstream.WriteLine("   PADDING-LEFT: 6px;")

txtstream.WriteLine("   FONT-WEIGHT: Normal;")

txtstream.WriteLine("   PADDING-BOTTOM: 6px;")

txtstream.WriteLine("   COLOR: white;")

txtstream.WriteLine("   PADDING-TOP: 6px;")

txtstream.WriteLine("   BORDER-BOTTOM: #999 1px solid;")

txtstream.WriteLine("   BACKGROUND-COLOR: navy;")

txtstream.WriteLine("   FONT-FAMILY: Cambria, serif;")

txtstream.WriteLine("   FONT-SIZE: 10px;")

txtstream.WriteLine("   text-align: left;")

txtstream.WriteLine("   white-Space: nowrap;")

txtstream.WriteLine(" Next")

```
txtstream.WriteLine("span")
txtstream.WriteLine("'")
txtstream.WriteLine("   BORDER-RIGHT: #999999 3px solid;")
txtstream.WriteLine("   PADDING-RIGHT: 3px;")
txtstream.WriteLine("   PADDING-LEFT: 3px;")
txtstream.WriteLine("   FONT-WEIGHT: Normal;")
txtstream.WriteLine("   PADDING-BOTTOM: 3px;")
txtstream.WriteLine("   COLOR: white;")
txtstream.WriteLine("   PADDING-TOP: 3px;")
txtstream.WriteLine("   BORDER-BOTTOM: #999 1px solid;")
txtstream.WriteLine("   BACKGROUND-COLOR: navy;")
txtstream.WriteLine("   FONT-FAMILY: Cambria, serif;")
txtstream.WriteLine("   FONT-SIZE: 10px;")
txtstream.WriteLine("   text-align: left;")
txtstream.WriteLine("   white-Space: nowrap;")
txtstream.WriteLine("   display: inline-block;")
txtstream.WriteLine("   width: 100%;")
txtstream.WriteLine(" Next")
txtstream.WriteLine("textarea")
txtstream.WriteLine("'")
txtstream.WriteLine("   BORDER-RIGHT: #999999 3px solid;")
txtstream.WriteLine("   PADDING-RIGHT: 3px;")
txtstream.WriteLine("   PADDING-LEFT: 3px;")
txtstream.WriteLine("   FONT-WEIGHT: Normal;")
txtstream.WriteLine("   PADDING-BOTTOM: 3px;")
```

```
txtstream.WriteLine("    COLOR: white;")
txtstream.WriteLine("    PADDING-TOP: 3px;")
txtstream.WriteLine("    BORDER-BOTTOM: #999 1px solid;")
txtstream.WriteLine("    BACKGROUND-COLOR: navy;")
txtstream.WriteLine("    FONT-FAMILY: Cambria, serif;")
txtstream.WriteLine("    FONT-SIZE: 10px;")
txtstream.WriteLine("    text-align: left;")
txtstream.WriteLine("    white-Space: nowrap;")
txtstream.WriteLine("    width: 100%;")
txtstream.WriteLine(" Next")
txtstream.WriteLine("select")
txtstream.WriteLine("'")
txtstream.WriteLine("    BORDER-RIGHT: #999999 3px solid;")
txtstream.WriteLine("    PADDING-RIGHT: 6px;")
txtstream.WriteLine("    PADDING-LEFT: 6px;")
txtstream.WriteLine("    FONT-WEIGHT: Normal;")
txtstream.WriteLine("    PADDING-BOTTOM: 6px;")
txtstream.WriteLine("    COLOR: white;")
txtstream.WriteLine("    PADDING-TOP: 6px;")
txtstream.WriteLine("    BORDER-BOTTOM: #999 1px solid;")
txtstream.WriteLine("    BACKGROUND-COLOR: navy;")
txtstream.WriteLine("    FONT-FAMILY: Cambria, serif;")
txtstream.WriteLine("    FONT-SIZE: 10px;")
txtstream.WriteLine("    text-align: left;")
txtstream.WriteLine("    white-Space: nowrap;")
```

```
txtstream.WriteLine("    width: 100%;")
txtstream.WriteLine(" Next")
txtstream.WriteLine("input")
txtstream.WriteLine("'")
txtstream.WriteLine("    BORDER-RIGHT: #999999 3px solid;")
txtstream.WriteLine("    PADDING-RIGHT: 3px;")
txtstream.WriteLine("    PADDING-LEFT: 3px;")
txtstream.WriteLine("    FONT-WEIGHT: Bold;")
txtstream.WriteLine("    PADDING-BOTTOM: 3px;")
txtstream.WriteLine("    COLOR: white;")
txtstream.WriteLine("    PADDING-TOP: 3px;")
txtstream.WriteLine("    BORDER-BOTTOM: #999 1px solid;")
txtstream.WriteLine("    BACKGROUND-COLOR: navy;")
txtstream.WriteLine("    FONT-FAMILY: Cambria, serif;")
txtstream.WriteLine("    FONT-SIZE: 12px;")
txtstream.WriteLine("    text-align: left;")
txtstream.WriteLine("    display: table-cell;")
txtstream.WriteLine("    white-Space: nowrap;")
txtstream.WriteLine("    width: 100%;")
txtstream.WriteLine(" Next")
txtstream.WriteLine("h1 '")
txtstream.WriteLine("color: antiquewhite;")
txtstream.WriteLine("text-shadow: 1px 1px 1px black;")
txtstream.WriteLine("padding: 3px;")
txtstream.WriteLine("text-align: center;")
```

txtstream.WriteLine("box-shadow: inSet 2px 2px 5px rgba(0,0,0,0.5), inSet -2px -2px 5px rgba(255,255,255,0.5);")

txtstream.WriteLine(" Next")

txtstream.WriteLine("</style>")